**HOW TO QUADRUPLE YOUR CHANCES
AT AN ATHLETIC SCHOLARSHIP**

LOOKING FOR A
FULL RIDE?

AN INSIDER'S RECRUITING GUIDE

RENEE LOPEZ, M.E.S.S.

POWERED BY

black card
B O O K S

Author: Renee Lopez, M.E.S.S.

Title: Looking for a FULL RIDE?

ISBN: 978-1-77204-699-1

Category: SPORTS & RECREATION/Coaching/General

Publisher: Black Card Books

Division of Gerry Robert Enterprises Inc.

Suite 214, 5-18 Ringwood Drive

Stouffville, Ontario, Canada, L4A 0N2

International Calling: +1 877 280 8736

www.blackcardbooks.com

....

LOOKING FOR A
FULL RIDE?

AN INSIDER'S RECRUITING GUIDE

RENEE LOPEZ, M.E.S.S.

POWERED BY

B O O K S

TABLE OF CONTENTS

ACKNOWLEDGMENTS

I want to thank many friends and family for their support during this long process of researching, interviewing, writing, editing, and marketing this book. I thank God in giving me this vision and the resilience to complete it, and to my parents, who encouraged and believed in me and in this project before I even believed I could complete it.

Thank you to those who contributed to this project. I appreciate the 65 college coaches and athletic directors and 25 other representatives who directly influence high school student-athletes and their families, who took the time to be interviewed. Thank you to the many who have edited and provided feedback on the project over the past few years.

Much appreciation to the friends and mentors who have supported both my coaching career and this entire book-writing journey, especially from Black Card Books, Catapult Entrepreneurs, Somos Church, Fellowship of Christian Athletes, the John Maxwell Team/DISC, the Jon Gordon Company, and the Positive Coaching Alliance. Your regular encouragement to push through the many challenges of birthing a project like this has made the difference, and I am eternally grateful.

I want to thank numerous friends and mentors who have influenced my sports career as both a student-athlete and coach, especially Frank and Louie Mateus, Gordy Poluyanskis, Ried Estus, Marlene Bjornsrud, Becky Burleigh, Matt Hisler, Tami Matheny, Adam Ritchie, Jennifer Calloway, Jim DeRose, Chris Neal, Steve Swanson, Kara Reber, and too many more to count!

An extra special thank you to all of the high school and youth coaches and parents who regularly remind me how much this resource is needed to educate families going through the college recruiting process. Thank you to all the young student-athletes I interact with regularly, especially my nephew Brett and niece Kate, who love athletics and inspire me to help educate future generations for the next level of sports competition.

CHAPTER 1

COLLEGE ATHLETIC RECRUITING OVERVIEW

I had just stepped onto the blacktop of the parking lot from the fields after watching several hours of competition when I overheard an abundance of confidence exuding from a high school student-athlete. This teenager was boldly stating to his (seemingly unconvinced) parents he was 100 percent sure he'd get a full athletic scholarship offer that week to continue playing his sport in college.

He continued stating his case: "All of those DI college coaches were there today. I assisted or scored every chance I had. With being All-Conference and after today, I AM GETTING A FULL RIDE. Trust me, they want me because I'll change their program!"

Was he talented? I watched part of his competition and can say, yes, he could play at the NCAA (National Collegiate Athletic Association) Division I level. Will he likely be offered a full athletic scholarship and "change their program"? Probably not.

I'm not so sure this player knew what being a college student-athlete entails, and why we call it the "recruiting process". Having spent 14 years as a College Coach at the NCAA Division I, II, III, and NAIA (National Association of Intercollegiate Athletics) levels, I was not surprised by the comments. I have heard many similar comments from potential recruits, their parents, and coaches.

As I started my car, I began thinking of an avenue to help provide perspective to student-athletes and their support systems about the realities of the college recruiting process. And my eavesdropping on this conversation is exactly where this insider's book began!

The purpose of this book is to help student-athletes and their support systems avoid common pitfalls, understand the realities of scholarship offers, and implement the best practices for getting recruited to play a sport in college.

THE STATS

To provide a true "insider's perspective" beyond my own 14 years of working as a college coach in NCAA Divisions I, II, III, and NAIA, (including 11 years as a Head Coach), three years as a High School Varsity Head Coach, two years serving as a NCAA Compliance Director, and a Director of Coaching for a youth travel club, I have interviewed more than 65 college coaches and athletic directors across the United States in 19 men's and women's college sports.

These interviews include college coaches and athletic directors from all three divisions of the NCAA. I also discussed best practices in recruiting with those coaches and administrators representing the National Association of Intercollegiate Athletics (NAIA), the National Christian College Athletic Association (NCCAA), the National Junior College Athletic Association (NJCAA), and the United States Collegiate Athletic Association (USCAA).

To provide comprehensive information, I also interviewed another 25 representatives who directly influence high school student-athletes and their families. These included high school administrators, college admissions and financial aid advising staff, college advisory program directors for multiple youth travel clubs, national executive directors for sports organizations, college faculty, and current and former NCAA legislative policy makers and compliance staff members.

TRENDS

Some common themes emerged from almost everyone involved in this two-year interview process. Most discussed the changing landscape in recruiting over the past 10 to 15 years, with a focus on earlier evaluation at summer camps and verbal commitments from student-athletes.

Several discussed the impact of advances in technology, social media, and how costly an inappropriate tweet or picture can be for a student's future. As Dan Talbot, Senior Coordinator of Athletics for all of Polk County in Florida, says, "I encourage students to watch what they put on social media. Don't let 100 characters [on Twitter] cost you $100,000 in scholarship money. It happens all the time."

Technological advances have also helped recruiters identify athletes outside of their local areas. Joshua Rebholz, Senior Associate Athletic Director at UCLA, addressed this pattern. "Almost every school recruits nationally and nearly all recruit internationally now. Before, most schools recruited locally, but with so much more information available to everyone online, athletes can be recruited from almost anywhere."

Many also addressed the recent and proposed legislative changes to create better boundaries for student-athletes to grow and develop without added pressure from outside representatives focused on placing athletes only at the NCAA DI level. Some stressed the need for more legislation for club coaches in youth organizations like the Amateur Athletic Union (AAU), Development Academies (DA), and the Elite Clubs National League (ECNL).

Shortly after her lacrosse team won the NCAA Division II National Championship at Florida Southern College, Head Coach Kara Reber stated, "We find the majority of our recruits from club tournaments run by our college coaching association or from kids coming to our camps or clinics on campus. It can be frustrating if club coaches are pushing their players to only look at NCAA Division I or scholarship dollars."

Coach Reber continued, "Ask my DII kids who just won a national championship if they regret their choice to look at our program. This was an amazing experience for them. Even though they are not playing DI or may not be on a full athletic scholarship, they were extremely successful."

Josh Snyder, Director of Athletics at NCAA Division II University of Sioux Falls, South Dakota, has spent 22 years in the sports industry. He agrees, "The biggest change is in all of the travel teams and tournaments. Kids travel all around to play in big tournaments, which gives coaches a chance to see them more easily, but also creates a false reality about future experiences."

John Diffley, Senior Associate Athletics Director at St. John's University, echoes the need for a shift in priorities in all of these events. "Youth sports are not [supposed to be] all about the scholarship, it [should be] about building lifelong skills, instilling values, creating memories, and friendships."

UNDERSTANDING THE BASICS

Another trend that emerged from interviews with more than 90 people who work directly with student-athletes was the emphasis on doing the necessary research early. A myriad of coaches recommended students start the process of marketing themselves to a large funnel of schools and not waiting until their senior year.

Steve Bluford works at St. Ignatius College Prep School in California. In addition to having coached football and track, he serves as the College Athletics Advisor. "The biggest mistakes I see are students starting the process too late, not really knowing what they want and thinking I will do the work for them. I tell them I am here to educate you on the process and ideally be invisible. This is about you and your future. You need to put in time to research colleges and know something about the program to make a good first impression."

College coaches were also quite clear. They are looking for talented student-athletes to help them win championships, as a coach's livelihood often depends on their team's performance. They often spoke of helping the students find the right college *fit* in terms of classroom size, location, academic rigor, major areas of study, affordability, and social environment. Student-athletes should be looking for a team culture fit as well.

Steve Swanson, the Head Women's Soccer Coach at the University of Virginia and the United States Women's National Team Assistant Coach, is no stranger to building championship teams. "Recruiting is about finding matches. It is not a right that everyone goes to college. Families need to find the place that meets the needs of the student-athlete and the needs of the program. Most of our student-athletes are on partial athletic scholarships, not full rides."

Coach Swanson continued, "No one says, 'I'm so happy at the school because I am on scholarship.' It's about the atmosphere and being like-minded. I feel it is important to look at the players as people first. Are they motivated, hungry to improve, and do they make their teammates better, no matter what their role? We want to help them reach their goals and are looking for players to buy into the culture of the team and then perform within a team environment."

SEEING THE BIGGER PICTURE

The bulk of college coaches and athletic directors encourage families not only to prioritize scholarship offers and the team's current success, but also to make a college decision with *"the broken leg test"* in mind, meaning, if the athletic opportunity no longer existed, would that college still be a good fit in all other aspects?

Coach Candace Fuller, who coaches at the University of California Riverside (NCAA Division I Track and Field, Throws coach), remarked, "Things can change from one meet to the next [in terms of success], but it doesn't change the reason you pick a program. *Fit* is the most important piece. Do you fit into the level you are chasing? Are you talented enough? Do you like the coach, the team, and the campus? Do not choose a college just because one school is offering you more money!"

Megan Kahn, who served for many years as a college basketball coach and now is the Executive Director for WeCOACH (formerly the Alliance of Women Coaches), reiterated these sentiments, "It's extremely important to remember the key to the whole recruiting process is finding the right *fit*... A parent and athlete should be interviewing a coach and school just as much as they are being recruited in return... When being recruited, don't get caught up in the adoration and flattery of the whole process."

It is essential to look beyond the beautiful aesthetics of campus facilities, athletic gear brand names, and scholarship offers. Families need to focus on academic programs, social atmosphere, safety, and career opportunities. It's also necessary to find a good fit with the current team members, coaches, faculty, and staff.

BEYOND THE X'S AND O'S

Recruiters are assessing the strengths and weaknesses of an athlete, but more importantly, they are evaluating the prospect's character and maturity to perform consistently at the next level academically and athletically. College coaches are observing how a recruit could positively contribute to the team culture. They are assessing how quickly an athlete could adapt to their new surroundings in a demanding athletic program, while being a team player who is coachable and comfortable with being in uncomfortable situations.

COLLEGE COACHES NEED THE WHOLE PACKAGE IN THEIR RECRUITS: DRIVE, INTELLIGENCE, CHARACTER, BUT MOST OF ALL, *MATURITY*.

Beyond athletic talent and academic rigor, recruiters' three most desired traits include resilience when facing challenges, discipline in daily habits, and ability to positively lead and impact others. College coaches need the whole package in their recruits: Drive, intelligence, character, but most of all, *maturity*. Mature athletes make a college coach's job much easier.

Jennifer Herron, the Head Women's Volleyball Coach at Clarion University, a NCAA Division II school in Pennsylvania emphasized, "I really like prospective student-athletes who have a clear vision and direction for their life with respect to how they want to make an impact within the team, at the university, and ultimately in their respective career path. Work ethic is a must. Problem solvers who welcome failure as their biggest teacher. We want students of the game who have a growth mindset."

At the University of Alabama, having championship programs is a way of life for Athletic Director Greg Byrne. He sees four key ingredients for building successful programs in a conference as challenging as the Southeastern Conference. "If they desire to play at this level, do they have the ability to stay focused on their academics, be a good teammate and leader, be coachable and not act like you have it all together, and make good decisions? Overall, we are looking for good people."

He also reiterated the struggle with current early commitments. "I hope the NCAA will continue to slow down the recruiting process with legislation regarding early commitments to allow these athletes to develop these attributes." Coaches need to measure these characteristics over time. If they make a large scholarship investment, they want to be sure an athlete has everything it takes beyond being an "All-Conference" level of talent. Throughout the entire recruiting process, it is imperative that student-athletes find ways to demonstrate each of these attributes to the potential college coach.

Finally, nearly all the college athletic directors and coaches referenced the pool of thousands of talented athletes they can choose from across the United States and internationally. These comments were especially emphasized by those in the Power 5 Conferences (Atlantic Coast Conference [ACC], Big Ten, Big 12, Pacific-12 [Pac-12], and SEC). If a teenager, parent, or high school/ youth coach takes a wrong step in the process, most colleges will gladly cross out a name on their list and walk over to the next field or court to find someone else equally as talented. This guide will help student-athletes reduce common mistakes made in the recruiting process.

BENEFITS AND DEMANDS OF BEING A COLLEGE STUDENT-ATHLETE

The Benefits

Dan Wood, Executive Director of the NCCAA, also urges families to look at the bigger picture in the opportunity to market college student-athletes for jobs. "Ten years from now, the acronyms NCAA, NAIA, or NCCAA will not matter and should not dictate the right fit for you."

However, when an employer looks at your resume ten years from now, they will be excited to see you have been a part of a college team.

Being a college student-athlete can provide great opportunities for a professional career in sports and in the boardroom. A recent study by the Drive Group of Fortune 500 CEOs reported that 95 percent played college sports. In a survey of 821 high-level executives, Ernst & Young found that 90 percent of women played sports, including 96 percent of executives. Yes, being a college-athlete can lead to success in a career other than playing professional sports! Lifelong lessons can be acquired being a college student-athlete such as time management, commitment, and being a good team player in the workforce.

As Richard Lapchick, Chair of the DeVos Sport Business Management Program at the University of Central Florida, states, "Playing a collegiate sport does so much for a person as far as personal and professional development. People in the industry and those heading graduate programs like myself like to hire and admit student-athletes because of the lessons they learn from that environment."

The Demands

Mr. Lapchick adds, "Being a student-athlete is such a big responsibility. They are role models for kids in the community and represent their peers, family, friends, coaches, the athletic department, the university as a whole, and the community." These are not roles to take lightly. A lot will be expected of a student-athlete. Great rewards come from great sacrifice.

Dan Campagna, Assistant Athletic Director at Emmanuel College in Massachusetts, says, "I want competitive kids who want to be first in their class, first on the field, and first in everything they do. Knowing a student-athlete is competitive, tells me they will always be up for a challenge."

Todd Lawton is the Head Men's and Women's Golf Coach at the University of South Carolina Upstate. "In golf, I need to understand how they play the game; it's not a game about others. You must understand your own means of excelling and competing. You need to have a history of being a self-starter and not one who needs to be babysat."

J. D. Ettore, who served nine years as an Athletic Director and currently leads Owens Community College in Ohio, offers his perspective. "Since I work at a community college, we expect our recruits to also help in the local communities. We expect them to reflect the values of our department... I tell them if we do not graduate you, we have failed. Being at a two-year institution, we always talk about academics first, because if the young athlete fails, they can kiss their academic or athletic scholarship goodbye. We tell the recruits that you may have been "the man" or "the woman" at your high school, and that may not be the case here. You will need to work in the classroom and on the field or court!"

While every level of college sports has specific restrictions on the amount of contact hours college coaches can have with their student-athletes, many teenagers do not realize what being a student-athlete is really like on a daily basis. It requires:

WILLINGNESS TO COMMIT.

- the willingness to give up time with friends to train harder than ever before, even if not a starter or with limited playing time;

- the discipline to eat properly, get sufficient sleep, and focus on recovery every day to optimize performance;

- the willingness to commit to sometimes be up at five a.m. for weight training;

- the desire to watch film and get treatments for injuries in the training room before and after practice;

- a commitment to attend study hall hours after practice; and

- the willingness to read books on mental training and leadership.

If a student-athlete cannot commit to these important aspects of playing at the next level, it may be better to research an intramural team or club level at the college. The Executive Director for the National Alliance for Youth Sports, John Engh, states, "Only an incredibly small portion of athletes will earn an athletic scholarship, so pushing and pressuring kids is not the way to go. All the alarming numbers regarding burnout and overuse injuries reveal a major problem today that can be traced back to disillusioned parents. Allow their love for the sport to evolve and if they have the skills and work ethic to be part of that elite group of scholarship athletes, they will be recognized."

He continues, "For that elite group that does have a chance of playing in college, we want to encourage parents to have a serious talk with their child to evaluate if this is what he or she truly wants. Often, kids are burned out and worn down by the sport by the time they finish high school and may just want to be a regular college student. There's nothing wrong with that!"

DIFFERENCES BETWEEN DIVISIONS (NCAA, NAIA, NCCAA, AND NJCAA)

There are a lot of misconceptions regarding the various levels of college athletics. As of the summer of 2019, there are 347 NCAA Division I, 309 Division II, and 442 Division III colleges. In addition, there are more than 525 junior colleges, 250 NAIA, and 81 USCAA athletic programs. NCAA DI schools are typically larger in size than the others.

Each governing body (NCAA, NAIA, NCCAA, NJCAA, and USCAA) has its own set of regulations for its institution, especially regarding recruiting, camps, campus visits, and overall communication. It is important to find out the most up-to-date recruiting timelines for a sport within each governing body by visiting their specific websites. Since many compliance rulebooks are hundreds of pages and constantly evolving, the following are generalities regarding the various levels.

The NCAA, NAIA, NCCAA, NJCAA, and USCAA have various rules depending on the sport and the student-athlete's graduation year. The NCAA has dead periods which are specific times of the year when a coach cannot meet a potential recruit on campus. In addition, the graduation year also dictates when NCAA coaches can contact a recruit and the frequency and types of contact they can have. Early in the high school years, coaches may often send a camp invite and a recruiting questionnaire to a prospective student-athlete. It is important not to misinterpret this as a limited expression of interest from a college coach, but instead recognize their restrictions in communication. The NAIA, NCCAA, NJCAA, and USCAA have less stringent rules, but it is important to understand the differences.

DON'T GET CAUGHT UP IN THE SCHOOL'S NAME OR THE DIVISION!

While NCAA Division I institutions typically offer a higher level of competition, athletic scholarships, and are usually larger in size than other schools, this is not always the case. It's extremely important to think about levels other than Division I as serious options. Assistant Athletic Director and Head Coach at Luther College, Russell Schoeweiler emphasizes, "Even though we don't offer athletic scholarships [at the DIII level], that doesn't mean that lessens the commitment by our players to our program. To play collegiate sports means to make a high-level commitment. It also doesn't mean that winning isn't important. DIII doesn't mean that we don't compete at a high level. Often, we are beating DII and DIs in scrimmages. What we can offer them is a full and real student-athlete experience; a great, high-level athletic experience paired with great academics."

Missy West was an integral member of the 1999 NCAA Women's Division I Basketball Championship at Duke University, later played professionally in Germany, and served 12 years as a collegiate coach at the DII and III levels. "Personally, I loved coaching at the DIII level. Certainly, there are financial benefits regarding playing DI and DII, and this may be a need for your family, depending on income. However, when it comes to your two or four years of happiness, there is no price tag for that."

She continued, "For many unfortunate kids, they allow this athletic scholarship to completely overshadow the most important aspect of the college experience and their education... not to mention their own personal values. They decide to pray everything will work out for the best and, sadly, this rarely happens."

Adam Ritchie was a high school coach for 12 years, worked in youth club programs for 15 years, and currently is the Head Men's Soccer Coach at New River Community College. He offers some great advice when starting the recruiting process, "Don't limit yourself to the top ten schools you have heard of on TV. There are a lot of schools out there with great programs. Look to see what fits your major and what sports program fits you best. A lot of parents and players want to make the best team at the best school. This does not always mean it is the *best fit* for the athlete."

Jody Martinez is the Head Women's Basketball Coach at Taylor University and has served 18 years in athletic administration and 27 years as a college coach. He shares this perspective: "If your child hasn't received a full ride offer to play basketball by the summer going into their junior year, then I tell parents that they need to look at NAIA schools as another option. In fact, their child will most likely have a better college playing experience at the NAIA level anyway."

Dr. Christopher J. Parker, CEO of the National Junior College Athletic Association, observes, "The NJCAA is 79 years old, and we focus on student success. We empower students to be their best and strive for their goals, whatever those may be. We value our 47 national championships and have passion for every student."

He continues, "The two-year level often provides many varied opportunities to include continued athletic development to reach their highest level of competition upon transferring, continued academic development if necessary, and if not on a full scholarship to a four-year college, then a student-athlete can earn a scholarship to an NJCAA college or at least save a lot of money (if needed)."

He adds, "Don't lock yourself in before you start. Have an idea in mind and look for colleges and opportunities that give you flexibility. That's what two-year colleges do. Also, don't say no to a college without an opportunity to at least see it."

Karin Gadberry is the former Senior Women's Administrator and the Head Women's Softball Coach at NCAA Division II New Mexico Highlands and now serves as the Head Softball and Women's Cross-Country Coach at Park University in Gilbert, Arizona. She believes that going the route of two-year colleges before transferring to a NCAA school is another option to explore. "Oftentimes, I filled my roster at DII with three to four junior college transfers. Sometimes you can get the benefit of more scholarship or playing time at that junior college level before transferring to a four-year school. I encourage you to explore all options. Be happy if given any opportunity, because probably 1,000 others would die for that opportunity. Don't get caught up in the name or the division!"

ATHLETIC SCHOLARSHIP REALITIES

Joe Niland, the Head Basketball Coach and Director of Athletics at the University of Mobile, stresses that very few athletic scholarships are available. "Receiving a college athletic scholarship is a difficult thing to do. It is not like moving from JV ball in high school to varsity. Moving to the college level is much more difficult and the opportunities are few."

It is important to note what scholarship allotments are available in a sport at the various levels. Some athletic scholarships cover tuition, room and board, books, and other associated cost-of-attendance fees. However, despite what is often portrayed in the media, not all of these are covered for every sport at every level.

Some sports are titled *equivalency sports*, meaning a certain allotment of dollars are spread across multiple team members, often resulting in partial athletic scholarships and limited "full rides". Other sports are categorized as *head-count* sports, meaning a certain number of student-athletes can be on scholarship, typically resulting in more full offers, but not necessarily.

It is important to know if the sport at the level being pursued is a head-count or equivalency sport. It is also important to note that not all programs are fully funded at the maximum numbers and often vary between men's and women's sports. For example, at the NCAA D1 level, women's soccer is an equivalency sport with 14 full scholarships allowed to be divided across the team roster versus NCAA D1 men's soccer with 9.9 full scholarships. In comparison, in NCAA D2 women's soccer the maximum is 9.9 and for men's soccer the maximum is 9.0 full scholarships. These scholarships allotments would be spread over the entire roster of 25–35 student-athletes on a team, often resulting in more partial scholarships versus full scholarships. These equivalencies describe the maximum amounts allowed, but many programs are not fully funded by the school's choice or by conference restrictions.

Other sports such as football, basketball, tennis, gymnastics, and women's volleyball are head-count sports, so they often will have more full tuition scholarships to offer than equivalency sports. It is important to consult the website of the appropriate governing body as head count and equivalencies vary across sports, gender, and levels of competition.

"Our biggest pet peeves in recruiting tend to be excessive scholarship expectations and dishonesty during the recruiting process about how much scholarship they need. The scholarship game is something we avoid, and we are upfront from the start about what we can afford and offer," comments Ryan Castle, the Head Coach of Women's Water Polo at Indiana University.

Jeanne Fleck, the Head Swim Coach at Fresno State, a NCAA DI university, says, "Ten percent of our team are walk-ons. We look for recruits who are honest, confident, goal oriented, and independent." Mike Schofield echoed the same for water polo. He was a College Coach for 31 years and recently retired from coaching at the Naval Academy. "About 100 kids across the United States and internationally get full rides in water polo."

Many athletic programs are *not* fully funded at the maximums allowed by the governing body. This is especially true in sports beyond football and basketball, even at the NCAA DI level. Many parents are often surprised to learn that their very talented student-athlete will be offered only a partial athletic scholarship of a few thousand dollars or even just a roster spot without any financial aid.

Emily Holsopple, North Carolina State University Rifle Head Coach, who previously spent four years at the US Olympic Training Center, concurs, "With 3.6 scholarship equivalencies, it can be quite difficult having to spread scholarships across typically seven to twelve student-athletes on our teams."

Tami Matheny, former NCAA DI and DII College Head Coach and Senior Women's Administrator, and current Mental Game Coach for many college and high school teams, shares this: "When I was coaching college tennis, everyone assumed we had every athlete on a full-ride athletic scholarship. In reality, we had zero on full rides, five percent were walk-ons, and ninety-five percent were on partial athletic scholarships."

Heath Eslinger, the Head Wrestling Coach at the NCAA DI University of Tennessee at Chattanooga, echoes the same sentiments about wrestling, "There are only 77 Division I schools for wrestling, so there aren't a lot of opportunities for athletes to participate at this level. Most schools also don't have the full allotment of scholarships (9.9 equivalencies) or a large recruiting budget, so the coach must be strategic in offering scholarships."

In most sports, the percentage of high school student-athletes who receive athletic scholarship offers (let alone full tuition dollars) is in the single digits.

"Right now, the highest percentage of high school players to have an opportunity to play a college sport is in women's hockey. You may not have a spot on the roster at your dream school, but there are enough programs compared to number of players out there that if you want to play, you more than likely will be able to find a fit to play," states Kelly Rider, the Head Women's Hockey Coach and Senior Women's Administrator at Northland College.

Conny Kirsch, the Recruiting Coordinator for the University of Central Florida [UCF] Rowing Team, says, "We must rely on walk-ons as our maximum scholarship numbers are twenty (per NCAA). Not every university in DI has twenty, but we do at UCF. Walk-ons can earn a scholarship depending on how they develop throughout their years of rowing."

CHAPTER 2

EXPLORING COLLEGE OPTIONS

STARTING THE PROCESS

If a high school student-athlete wants to play in college, and with so few athletic scholarships available, where on Earth does a student-athlete start?

Tod Creneti has spent 26 years as a high school and college football coach. He recently led the St. Stephens Episcopal School in Bradenton, Florida, to back-to-back state championships, and sent more than 50 student-athletes to play in college on athletic scholarships. "The biggest mistakes I see are families paying for recruiting services and also using their own evaluation of their child's talent as the gold standard. Families need to be honest about the talent and abilities of their student-athlete [and how that translates at the college level]. Athletes should dial in on which schools meet their academic and social interests, and then begin to build a relationship with the coach who recruits their area."

WHEN AND HOW DO WE START?

The most frequent question asked during recruiting seminars is, "When do we start the process so we can ensure the student-athlete 'gets seen' by college coaches?"

Erik Ellefsen is the Academic College Counselor at Valley Christian High School in California. He has served as a baseball and basketball coach for more than 15 years, and says, "For about seventy-five percent of our athletes, I recommend they have some film from playing a full season of a varsity sport to start the process. However, in some sports, waiting that long could be too late to secure an athletic scholarship or even roster position at the next level. It varies by sport, the level of competition, and by programs."

During their freshman and sophomore years, student-athletes should create and contact via email a list of 20 to 40 colleges. (This list will get reduced depending on college coach interest.) This initial contact list should include various levels. It is essential for families to evaluate three major criteria about the college to create this large list:

1. Academic and Social Atmosphere

Choosing a specific major can be a daunting task; instead, ask what are two to three subject areas the student-athlete enjoys and might want to continue to pursue in college? Doing some basic Internet searches can yield multiple resources to narrow down schools offering a potential major. Many liberal arts colleges offer pre-med, education, and business degrees, but you may need to do a bit more research to find colleges with marine biology, engineering, athletic training, and graphic design. Identifying a few subject areas of interest can help you narrow the field for further research on athletic programs.

Finding a fit academically and socially really boils down to what type of environment the student-athlete can best succeed in: *As a large fish in a small pond versus a small fish in a large pond?* Is it better for the student-athlete to know professors well in smaller classes, or would they be able to handle a lecture hall for introductory courses with possibly 100 to 500 students in the class?

FIND A FIT FOR YOU TO BE SUCCESSFUL ACADEMICALLY THAT WILL HELP YOUR FUTURE CAREER.

2. Career Opportunities

Exploring what the school offers for internships, study abroad, and other practicum experiences is also an essential step. Is the college connected to a major corporation enabling them to regularly place their business majors in internships? Are there options to enhance journalism skills through a local newspaper or TV station? For a major in sports management, can the student get experience in their athletic department? Investigating these options *prior* to focusing on a roster spot offer can help decipher which programs might provide the right career steps.

Some institutions located in smaller towns may have great connections with local businesses but may not have as many options for getting experience. Large cities may offer a wealth of opportunities, but without college connections for internships, there may be heavy competition. Thinking through a career beyond athletics means investigating areas that could enhance a résumé!

3. Location

While the size and setting of the college can influence career opportunities, the physical location of the school is extremely important as well. With an outdoor sport, the type of weather will be important. There's a big difference between playing an outdoor sport in Florida's humidity and daily afternoon storms versus Denver's high altitude. And it's much warmer weather in Florida for spring sports such as softball, baseball, and lacrosse than states farther north!

When thinking through the location of potential schools, it is crucial to know if a car is needed to get around on campus or in the local city. Some larger schools will have bus transportation to get to a grocery store or even to some internships.

Finally, it is important for student-athletes to ponder how far they really want to be from home. Jessika Caldwell, a former standout at Baylor University, has served as a DII Assistant and Head College Coach and now is the Head Women's Basketball Coach and Assistant Chaplain at Valor Christian High School near Denver, Colorado. Her coaching has resulted in championship teams at both the college and the high school level. She advises, "Take a map of the USA and decide where you want to live. Also think about the cost to fly there, come home for breaks, and for having your family travel to see you play. I also highly encourage choosing some top "reach"/ dream schools, some realistic schools, and some safety colleges."

ACADEMICS AS FIRST PRIORITY

When students are creating their initial lists of colleges, they should also examine the current team's majors and involvement in extracurricular activities. It is important to see that the team's GPA is high and has a diverse set of academic majors (and not just a trend of pushing a student-athlete toward "easier" majors to keep them eligible).

Coach Jennifer Calloway spent 23 years as a Head Women's College Volleyball Coach in South Carolina. She states, "Education is what they are there for in the first place. We want them to graduate. Academics are important. My programs always follow a higher standard of academics than for the regular student and that includes study hall during season, based off their GPA."

It is essential to understand what amount of emphasis the college coach and program place on academics. In addition, college coaches want to know that academics are a priority to the prospective student-athlete, not just the parent. In marketing to a coach, emphasize that getting an education is what is driving the desire to look at this college, not just the sport.

Eddie Payne coached men's college basketball for 43 years at many colleges, including Oregon State University and East Carolina University. He most recently retired as the Head Men's Basketball Coach from NCAA Division I University of South Carolina Upstate, where many of his players were featured on ESPN. He believes, "If there isn't a balance between academics and athletics, we were probably not going to recruit them. We wanted to know the student-athlete had their priorities straight. This was our focus!"

Jason Dowiak, the Head Women's Soccer Coach at the University of Massachusetts, agrees: "Academics is our focus initially. We want to recruit kids we know take care of themselves in the classroom, and therefore we know we have a more mature player that likely won't fall into eligibility issues."

University of Florida Athletic Director Scott Stricklin offers this advice to student-athletes: "The college needs to be setting you up for life, even if you continue to play professionally. It is important to not put the cart before the horse. Find a place you can be led and pushed with solid people who help you for life. The key is everyone can have the opportunity to use their degrees."

Stephen Watson, the Director of Athletics of DI Loyola University Chicago, advises parents, "Make sure your child truly loves the sport. Division I athletics requires a huge commitment and is extremely difficult if you don't truly love your sport. Rather than focus on what 'level' you want to play at, look at what kind of school you want to attend academically."

THE "BROKEN LEG TEST"

Nearly every coach and athletic director interviewed for this book discussed the value of fully getting to know the university beyond the athletic program. Imagine this scenario:

You have trained all summer prior to your freshman year and are in the best shape of your life. You are excited for the first intrasquad scrimmage. Your name is in the starting lineups, and your stomach starts to turn. The competition begins and in the first ten minutes of play, your shoelaces get tangled. You tumble to the ground and land awkwardly.

The certified athletic trainers do some initial evaluation. Maybe it's a broken leg or the dreaded torn ACL in the knee. The college season is probably now being redirected to possible surgery, rehabilitation, and cheering from the sidelines.

So, the "broken leg test" is exactly this scenario played out... If the unthinkable injury happens, is this still the right college? The student-athlete should evaluate the list of questions below and research any that they cannot definitively say *yes* to immediately about a first-choice college. Do not let a large athletic scholarship offer dictate the four-year choice without thinking these through:

1. Does the school have the academic programs that will help me pursue my career and get a job?

2. Are the right academic support systems (such as tutoring) available on campus to help a student-athlete be successful?

3. Am I able to get accepted to the university with my current test scores and GPA?

4. Will I also be eligible at this level for the NCAA with my GPA in core courses?

5. Will the college social atmosphere promote successful time management for balancing academics, athletics, and social life?

6. Is the distance between college and home right for me?

7. How will I get to a grocery store or the movies if I don't have a car?

8. Is the college located in a setting in which I can feel comfortable (city, suburbs, country)?

9. Do I feel safe being on this campus? What procedures are in place for coming home from the library late at night or restricting access to a dorm?

10. Do the living arrangements (residence hall, campus apartment, etc.) feel comfortable?

11. Will the coach challenge me to grow and evolve as a student and person first, and then as an athlete? If the coach leaves, do I still love the school enough to stay there?

12. When I visit with the team, do I mesh with the current athletes?

13. Is the overall financial package affordable for me to attend this university?

"DI ON THE BRAIN"

Numerous college coaches have observed how some student-athletes only research DI programs. Yet it can actually stifle the recruiting process if they only have "DI on the Brain". Not all talented high school student-athletes can play or receive scholarship offers at the DI level. It is important not to limit opportunities and to contact all different levels of competition with schools that meet "the broken leg test" criteria.

Jane Loyd, Assistant Women's Volleyball coach at the University of California San Diego, described her experience, "Having coached in both NCAA DI and DII, I think it is important to look beyond the recognizable name of a school and conference. Division II and III schools offer a unique balance enabling student-athletes to have a well-rounded college experience. They get the best of both worlds: They are student-athletes, but they are allotted time to be students while still enjoying college activities and organizations outside of their sport. Many DII and III athletic programs are located at phenomenal academic institutions!"

Dr. Sue Nyhus is the Head Women's Golf coach at Utah Valley University. She believes "the division matters much less than your priorities. Your priority should be in seeing if a strong academic program is available. And then your second priority should be if you have an opportunity to compete, and not just be on the roster."

Daven Bond, the Head Softball Coach at DII Regis University, says, "Many DI programs won't allow student-athletes to choose a highly demanding major. I have six girls who are nursing majors. I even have one who transferred from a DI to play here for us because she figured out, she can't balance the demanding curriculum level and DI athletics. DII programs also allow professors to really get to know the student-athlete. Professors are not afraid to call me if there is an academic issue. The professors are hands-on. You just don't get that at the bigger universities! DII really is a tight-knit community experience."

Erin Coppernoll, the Head Women's Soccer Coach at University of Wisconsin Oshkosh, echoed the same sentiments, "An athlete should consider NCAA Division III as it is an environment that provides balance for the student-athlete. Division III athletics provides a good template for balancing multiple roles in life, which all of us as adults need to do!"

RESEARCHING CHRISTIAN COLLEGES

Not all Christian colleges are the same. They vary in terms of denomination, lifestyle requirements, emphasis on chapel attendance, and staff requirements to integrate faith into all aspects of academic and extracurricular activities.

Daniel Stange, Athletic Director and the Head Baseball Coach at the University of St. Katherine, shares that being a Christian is not a requirement for some Christian colleges, so it is essential to fully research the school. He says, "At a Christian university, being a Christian is one of the first things that we will look for, but it is not required. Being a person with good morals and high-quality character are at the top of the list. We are a school that stresses development of the person more than winning, both on and off the field."

Jeff Wardlaw is the Head Women's Soccer Coach at NCAA DIII Greenville University in Illinois. He encourages student-athletes to explore a college in depth. "Figure out the intentionality of the school. Many of them are Christian in name only. When visiting campus, ask educated questions. How is faith integrated in the sport? Is there an idea of playing for a Higher Purpose?"

He adds, "In our program, we do a devotional before a game and practice. We also do a mandatory Bible study in the off-season, sometimes a worship service before meetings, and pray with the opposing team after a match no matter what the result."

Having worked in Christian colleges for four years, I know it can be an amazing experience for the right student-athlete. However, student-athletes often do not have a very clear picture of what this 'fit' would actually be like in daily life academically, athletically, and socially. Make sure you fully research the college, attend a chapel, meet with current student-athletes, faculty, and staff.

—Renee Lopez

Research the following areas when visiting a Christian College campus:

1. **What percent of the students in the school are committed Christians? On the team?**

This is an essential question as some colleges will run a 70/30 (or 80/20) percentage of Christians to non-Christians, while other schools will have 100 percent of their team members as committed believers. These percentages will dictate much of the atmosphere of a campus and its sports teams. Another great way to investigate these priorities is to evaluate the admissions essay requirements. Do they ask a general question about a student's spiritual background or about a specific date of accepting Christ?

2. **What are the campus and athletic department expectations that impact daily life and the campus culture?**

It is imperative for student-athletes to understand the overall lifestyle policies before committing to a specific college. It is essential to know policies regarding chapel attendance, drinking, swearing, community service, pregnancy, retreat attendance, and Bible studies.

3. **Attend a chapel.**

Do not miss this as it will be one of the greatest indicators of the spiritual climate of the college. Are the worship services student or faculty led? How engaged are the students? What emphasis does the school place on deep spiritual growth? Is it only surface level?

4. **Ask what local churches the student-athletes and coaches attend in the area.**

Try to visit one during a campus visit or watch a service online.

5. **Investigate how the coaches are fed spiritually.**

It is hard for them to pour out from an empty cup! Since travel often prevents coaches from attending weekend services, a healthy athletic department will focus on spiritually developing their coaches.

6. Ask the current student-athletes and coaches about their vision for sports ministry inside of their team.

Ask them what takes place spiritually at meetings, practice, and on competition days. Do they start and end each gathering with prayer? Are these coach or student led? How do teammates resolve conflict?

7. Ask team members about their vision for sports ministry outside of their team.

Is there a healthy focus on both winning and outreach ministry? Do they pray with opposing teams no matter the result?

8. Ask the coaches about their vision for serving in the local community and if they do any international sports ministry trips.

Each of these elements will help a family gather a more complete picture about the school environment and determine if it is the right *fit* for the student-athlete. Remember, not all Christian colleges are alike, so it is essential to fully research how integrated Christ is into the school culture and athletic department.

Finally, as Dan Wood, Executive Director of the NCCAA, states, "The last thing we want is all Christian kids at Christian colleges. If you want/can play at a top level and are spiritually mature, go and be the salt and light in the program!"

CHAPTER 3

UNDERSTANDiNG THE ELIGIBILITY CENTERS

To play at the NCAA Division I, II, or NAIA level, It is necessary to complete paperwork for the Eligibility Center (formerly called the Clearinghouse). There are separate Eligibility Centers for the NCAA and for the NAIA. It is important to note that NJCAA, USCAA, and NCAA Division III do not have the same requirements to play as NCAA Division I or II (refer to their websites for requirements).

The number one misconception most families have regarding eligibility is thinking that a student-athlete who is accepted to the college or university is automatically eligible to play. This is not necessarily true. Student-athletes should take the initiative to make sure everything is on track. (This is not the responsibility of the college coach, school counselor, or high school/club coach.)

RECOMMENDATIONS

1. Investigate EARLY in high school if the student is on track with core courses!

Being eligible to play in college is not based on the overall high school GPA. Instead, it is based on completing a set of core courses with a specific GPA. These core courses are determined by the NCAA and NAIA. It is crucial to verify the coursework is on track with the high school and with the NCAA and NAIA very early in the student's high school career.

I once had a DI student-athlete who never checked out her core courses GPA with the NCAA and school counselor early in her high school career. After she graduated from high school in June (just two months before she was to start her freshman season of competition at the college), the NCAA Compliance Director at the university saw an error on her files. He triple-checked because she had higher than a 4.0. Since she placed extremely high in academics in middle school, she opted to skip a course in high school. However, she had not completed all the core courses needed for eligibility. Yes, you read that right . . . Her GPA was greater than a 4.0, yet she was not eligible.

There is nothing worse than a student-athlete finding out after graduating high school with a 4.0 GPA that she did not complete all the correct courses to be eligible to play in college! The only resolution was that this 4.0 student-athlete had to take two online courses that summer before college. This girl had worked her heart out throughout her high school year but had to attend summer school to be eligible for her season in August. Double-check everything!

2. Do not wait until senior year to register!

As this story illustrates, student-athletes need to register for both Eligibility Centers early on in their high school career. It's best to register during freshman year for both the NCAA and the NAIA Eligibility Center and include those ID numbers in emails to coaches.

3. Send official copies of academic transcripts directly to the Eligibility Centers!

Make sure OFFICIAL transcripts get sent directly to the Eligibility Centers (this can be done digitally). Do not just make a copy of grades and mail them. In addition, a final copy of transcripts needs to be sent after graduation from high school. Be sure to request this prior to summer as many clerical staff are on vacation then, which could cause delays.

4. Send official ACT/SAT test results directly to the Eligibility Centers!

Even though test scores can be requested after the fact, it is a much easier process to include the specific codes for the NCAA and NAIA when registering for the tests. When the College Board asks which colleges to have test scores sent to, add in 9999 for the NCAA and 9876 for the NAIA.

Another student-athlete of mine had a common first and last name (think Sarah Johnson). She had a 30 on her ACT and a 4.0+ GPA. She had taken all the right courses, but she kept showing up as ineligible. It turned out that her files were crossed with another person with the identical name who had a 14 ACT and a 2.0 GPA. Luckily, we caught it before she had to miss a scrimmage or game, but it was not a fun process to resolve!

DOUBLE-CHECK EVERYTHING!

5. Complete the amateurism questions! Twice!

Questions related to amateurism will be included in the registration with the Eligibility Center. They are basically trying to determine if a student-athlete has been paid to play (or rewarded) beyond normal travel expenses. This has zero impact for most student-athletes, but completing these steps is necessary. It often can come into play for international student-athletes or those who have competed overseas, especially in tennis, golf, and soccer.

In the spring of senior year (for the NCAA, after April 1), the student-athlete will need to go back in and complete some questions and request final amateurism certification. Basically, this is just a follow-up on the original registration to verify the original answers.

HOMESCHOOL CONSIDERATIONS

Families should also register with the Eligibility Centers under the specific area designated for homeschoolers. It is essential for homeschool families to start this process early (in what would be the traditional ninth grade year) because the Core Course requirements can often be quite overwhelming for a parent to plan out. The NCAA website also has a *Home School Toolkit* to help families through the process.

Scott Larson, Senior Associate Director of Athletics at Lubbock Christian University in Texas, has previously worked in NCAA Compliance at both the DI and the DII level. He says, "Homeschool requirements are typically the same. However, it is a bit more complicated as the NCAA will evaluate each course on its own merit by the homeschooling accreditation agency in the home state."

FREE
FACEBOOK GROUPS

 Educating Parents of HS Athletes on the College Recruiting Process

 Mindset & Leadership Lessons 4 Athletes & Coaches/Teachers

 Athletic Recruiting Education for Principals, Counselors, & ADs

 Club/High School Coaches Learning about the College Recruiting Process

 Christian Competitors

Visit www.rlopezcoaching.com for 40+ blogs

To Book Coach Renee for live events, email info@lookingforafullride.com

CHAPTER 4

MARKETING TO COLLEGE COACHES

CONTACTING COACHES

A college coach's email inbox can become completely full, especially in the weeks leading up to a college showcase. Steve Swanson, Head Women's Soccer Coach at the University of Virginia, says, "We receive 250 to 500 emails in the weeks leading up to a tourney. We will get more than 1,000 for any given recruiting class. At an event, we will likely watch 25 to 50 specific recruits." It is essential to find ways to stand out from the crowd with personalized contact. There is no worse first impression than an email address that is not professional.

I literally had someone email me with her address including bringingsexyback##. I didn't know how to respond. The ironic part was that she had a high GPA and excellent test scores. However, after reading the first two sentences of the email from this address, I didn't even watch her recruiting video.

—Renee Lopez

Laura-Ann Lane is the Head Field Hockey Coach and Senior Woman's Administrator at DIII Gwynedd Mercy University in Pennsylvania. "One of my biggest frustrations is receiving emails without proper spelling or, even worse, in tweet-speak abbreviations." Parents can help proofread, but many college coaches will simply delete emails written by a parent. Student-athletes need to be making the initial contact.

Personalize Emails

They also need to find ways to stand out positively in their emails. Dan Kenneally has been a college coach for more than 20 years. He currently coaches Spartanburg Methodist College, a member of the NJCAA, located in South Carolina. "One of my biggest pet peeves is when a recruit sends an email addressing the wrong coach or college name because they are just copying and pasting emails to multiple colleges. I encourage student-athletes to use the website to demonstrate they have done their research about the specific school. Discuss a recent exciting win, a team community service project, and potential academic interests."

James Schrenk is the Recruiting Coordinator, Quarterbacks Coach, and Offensive Coordinator for Augustana University Football in South Dakota, and he adds, "If we are in your list of schools, you need to come after us. Do not pay someone like a recruiting service to do it for you. Go actively get yourself recruited through emails, phone calls, and letters. Don't just pay to have your emails sent to college coaches with the same exact form letter the college coach gets for 100–200 kids that month!"

Becky Carlson, the Head Rugby Coach at Quinnipiac University, agrees, "I like personalized emails and do not like template emails from scouting agencies and recruiting services." Most coaches discourage the typical mass emailing that comes from these types of recruiting services. They want to hear directly from the student-athlete (and not a company they paid to do it for them).

STAND OUT FROM THE CROWD.

New Mexico State Assistant Football Coach for Tight Ends and Special Teams Ronnie Pentz encourages recruits to differentiate themselves, but also to provide essential information. "I get tons of personalized emails per day. Don't just link to a recruiting service. Make my life easier. Many emails do not include everything I need. Provide your phone number, graduation year, contact information, and unofficial transcripts."

The majority of coaches want the following in initial emails from recruits:

1. Full name of student-athlete and parents

2. Contact info: Mailing address, email address, and cell phone number

3. Graduation year

4. High school/club coach contact information

5. Position, team colors, and jersey number

6. Current academic information

7. Academic major interests

8. Upcoming game schedule

9. Link to player's résumé and video footage

10. What is most appealing about the university?

You can download a FREE *Special Report: Strategies to Emailing a College Coach* and find more information about educational webinars, live seminars, blogs, and Facebook groups for parents and coaches. Visit www.rlopezcoaching.com

Attach a Player Résumé

Create a one-page player résumé to attach to the email (so a college coach can print and carry it with them while attending your competition versus searching through hundreds of emails). It should include the aforementioned list, an updated headshot, social media links, community involvement, academic and athletic achievements, personal and athletic references, and basic statistics. Do not send files that are over 1 MB as they can clog many college coaches email inboxes.

Understand the Value of High School Statistics

It is important to market athletic abilities to a college coach, but do not send pages of statistics for them to wade through. They will want to see a potential recruit in person or speak to a reference who understands the level of competition. Frank Marcinek has been the Assistant Athletic Director and Head Men's Basketball Coach at Susquehanna University for 13 years. He advises families to keep perspective as far as offering information to college coaches. "High-level statistics in high school are only a small piece of the puzzle, not the whole puzzle. Every kid is a captain, but that doesn't necessarily mean they are a great leader. I try to usually talk to someone who knows about the kid and the level of competition."

In some sports such as track, cross-country, swimming, tennis, and golf, the recruiting process may be a bit more definitive based on specific standards and rankings, but integrity still matters. Katie Robinson is the current Associate Head Coach for Swimming and Diving at Northwestern University in Illinois and was formerly the Head Coach at Tulane University in Louisiana for five seasons. "We are times-based in recruiting, which will get your foot in the door. Some athletes could possibly win their state meet and still not have recruitable times. However, it's up to a recruit's character for us to open the door for them."

Don't lie or exaggerate. Jason Davis has been a Head and Assistant Track and Field College Coach for over 15 years and agrees, "Statistics can be very helpful for us in recruiting. But if you don't meet the standards expected, do not lie. With stats readily available on the Internet, I highly recommend you simply don't do it."

Timing is Everything

Asking for an athletic scholarship in an initial email is like asking someone to get married on a first date. It likely will not turn out well for the relationship. College coaches have so many student-athletes to choose from that they need to do their due diligence in researching a recruit's academic background, athletic ability, and character. As Coach Becky Carlson of Quinnipiac observes, "Student-athletes who write one-liners asking solely about scholarships prior to telling me anything about themselves are likely not to warrant a second look." Don't hurt your chances by asking the coach to commit with scholarships too early in the process!

Frequency

"There are only so many hours in a day for a coach to reply to recruits. I appreciate contact once every couple of months from freshmen or sophomores. With a junior, I like once every month, and with seniors, every couple of weeks," states Matt Hisler, the Head Women's Soccer Coach at Johnson and Wales University in Charlotte. Student-athletes should not feel the pressure to email every single week, but it is essential for college coaches to consistently hear from a recruit.

CREATING RECRUITING VIDEOS

An essential element of initial emails to a coach should include a link to a video showing the student-athlete's abilities. If the student-athlete is in a team sport, coaches want to see game film, but most do not want to see an entire game. It needs to be edited. *However, it is important to note this does not require spending hundreds of dollars on a professional video service!*

Most coaches interviewed stated they valued video clips as a first step in the recruiting process. It's acceptable to put a video together, upload it on YouTube, Hudl, or QU Athletes and send the link.

Important tips:

1. *An initial video should be five to eight minutes long.*

    College coaches get tons of videos each week. The specific type of video college coaches desire can vary by sport, but for most team sports, the video is often the first step in getting a coach to come see you play live. They rarely will watch more than the first five minutes, so make sure those first plays represent your best competition footage.

    For more individualized sports, it may be more of a coach's preference. Leslie Payne, the Head Cross Country and Track and Field Coach at DIII Meredith College, says, "I like to see their running form throughout a race (beginning, middle, end) as form plays a key part in performance."

2. *Show 30 seconds before and after the play.*

    Provide multiple clips including 30 seconds before and 30 seconds after the student-athlete makes a play for constant run of play sports like field hockey, soccer, rugby, basketball, and lacrosse. The recruiters want to see how the play was set up (which impacted the decisions made), as well as what happened after the play.

3. *For team sports, show a large playing surface.*

   Make sure there's a wide view showing a lot of the playing surface and others nearby, especially for field games like lacrosse, soccer, football, rugby and field hockey. Even for indoor sports like volleyball and basketball, most coaches are looking for your decision-making both with and without the ball. When the film only shows the athlete up close, it limits the opportunity to evaluate technical skills versus tactical decision-making. This is one of the biggest mistakes a recruit can make for videos.

4. *Help coaches quickly identify you from your teammates.*

   In the student's email to the coach, it is imperative to label the team's color, position being played, and jersey number. The athlete should wear something that identifies them quickly (if allowed in the league) such as a wrist/headband, bright-colored cleats, a hair braid, or other visible markings. This makes it easier for a coach to see and quickly identify the athlete, as jersey numbers aren't always clear from a distance.

5. *Include contact information at the beginning and end.*

   Always include name, high school/travel club, graduation year, and email address at the beginning and end of the video. Coaches get hundreds of videos in a span of a few weeks. Including this information will help a coach differentiate you from the others!

6. *Stay Safe!*

   After uploading the video online, make sure you create a password to protect it on YouTube since personal information is now included. Once completing the uploads, insert the link and any passwords in the email to the coach. This is essential to protect your identity!

7. *Differentiate yourself.*

Adding background music is fine, but again, this doesn't have to be a major production. Sam Wolinski was the Head Women's Volleyball Coach at Eastern Illinois University, and she now helps families understand the recruiting process. She emphasizes that recruits should "choose music that doesn't overtake the video. Also, cussing on the video music doesn't go over well. The video should be to spark our interest in seeing you live!"

Go above and beyond to make this first impression the best you can. A potential recruit with some guitar skills once included an original song in the background. Another student-athlete sent a letter via snail mail with her video on a DVD and included bags of popcorn to enjoy. Demonstrate how you recovered quickly after making a huge mistake or your team was scored on. Find ways to stand out and be remembered from the hundreds of emails and videos coaches receive every month.

8. *Mute the conversations.*

Coaches really don't want to hear parents on the sidelines. Ask whoever is filming the video to turn the microphone off while filming or use music to cover up the crowd's conversations.

9. *Follow up with the coach.*

For juniors or seniors, it is especially important to send a follow-up email to the coach about seven to ten days after you sent your initial email to determine their interest level. If they are in their championship season, it's better to give them more like 10 to 14 days as they are likely swamped with traveling for their season. It is imperative you only ask for feedback on the student-athlete's potential as a recruit for them. (Do not ask about scholarships at this initial stage in the process.)

BEST SOCIAL MEDIA MARKETING TECHNIQUES

While almost every high school student-athlete is on social media multiple times a day, they often do not realize how many college coaches evaluate their sites during the recruiting process. Many athletic scholarship dollars have been lost by recruits demonstrating their immaturity on social media. It's extremely important for every student-athlete to examine what they have personally posted as well as pictures and videos they are tagged in.

However, there's a way to get a positive head start on the recruiting process with specific types of posts college coaches are looking for from their future athletes.

What student-athletes should post on social media related to athletics:

1. Pictures and videos with your teammates hanging out and having clean fun.

College coaches want to see that you really enjoy hanging around your team. They love to see you and your team belting at the top of your lungs your favorite pregame pump-up song (clean lyrics, of course!) and the dance party after a big win in the locker room. If your team beat a top-ranked team, post that buzzer beater video that hit the local news cycle. Show that you have a huge passion for athletics!

2. Positivity even after a tough loss.

Every team faces adversity. Maybe it's an injury, a broken-down bus, the loss of a huge lead in the ninth inning, or uniforms that shrunk. On social media, use the opportunity to post an inspirational phrase, Bible verse, or personal way of making lemonade out of lemons.

Discuss how great a work ethic your team had even when they faced giving up that lead. Demonstrate to the college coach that you can bounce back from challenging situations.

3. **Shout-outs for a teammate, coach, or teacher who inspired or encouraged you.**

This can be an effective tool for having college coaches see you in a positive light if it's *authentic*. What if you did a Twitter shout-out to the team equipment managers? What about acknowledging a captain on Instagram who has shown great leadership? Each *authentic*, positive post you make can demonstrate that you are the type of person a coach wants in their program!

4. **Commitment to academics.**

While discussing that daunting Algebra II test does not usually rate high on the most exciting topics to discuss on social media, it could win you some points with college recruiters. You can even use hashtags to demonstrate you have your priorities in line (ex. #mygradesmatter).

5. **A life outside of your sport.**

College coaches want to find student-athletes they can enjoy being with for the next four years and who bring something to the long bus rides. They want to see your character and values. Post pictures of your family and friends going to a theme park or helping pack care packages for hurricane victims. If you love to play the guitar, record a video of you playing a few notes. Maybe discuss how you helped with a church Vacation Bible School or volunteering at a children's hospital. Include anything that shows you are a balanced person!

STANDING OUT AT A
COLLEGE SHOWCASE TOURNAMENT

Many student-athletes believe that their high school seasons are the best way to get seen by a college coach. However, in most team sports (beyond football), club or travel ball teams often provide unique opportunities for coaches to see hundreds of potential recruits over the course of one weekend.

Jennifer Herron, the Head Volleyball Coach at Clarion University, states, "I love that we can go into a convention center with 100+ courts to a national-level tournament and see athletes from all over the country competing over the course of a three-day weekend. It helps in being able to identify more athletes within a smaller time frame. I could watch a single athlete that we are serious about play in a minimum of seven matches and potentially more. In that time, you can identify several things that encompass that athlete, especially how they react to winning, losing, making errors, getting feedback from coaches, and how they interact with family members and teammates."

Heather Brink, the Head Coach of Women's Gymnastics at the University of Nebraska, agrees, "There are several regions that will host a college showcase for the athletes within that region. We attend these showcases to watch a lot of gymnasts from several different clubs to identify the prospective student-athletes (PSAs) for whom we might potentially schedule a personal gym visit. It also allows us the opportunity to see the coach in action with several athletes. Since we are recruiting at a very young age, we place a lot of trust in a coach to either maintain the athlete's level of gymnastics or increase the level of the athlete's gymnastics. In addition, we need to trust the coach to be safe and keep the student-athlete healthy."

It is also essential for recruits to know that college coaches are always watching during these events even after the competition is over. Laura-Ann Lane, the Head Field Hockey Coach and Senior Women's Administrator at NCAA Division III Gwynedd Mercy University, encourages student-athletes to be aware of their communication at these large showcase events. "They must be a good person first and foremost. There are 30 fields at a huge recruiting event. If your mom just walked all the way over to give you a sports drink, and you throw it back at her because it's the wrong flavor, you can go and play for someone else. If you are rude to your parents or your coaches, you are not the right fit for us."

Jay Rayner is the Technical Director of the Pride Soccer Club and helps multiple student-athletes every year with the college recruiting process. He shares, "One of the most important aspects is educating players on what the process looks like, the timelines and pitfalls. And truly explaining what they should be doing when preparing for showcases is extremely important. This is not a cattle auction. It's a life decision that will have a profound impact on your future. Take the time to do your research. Choose the school, not necessarily the coach, and then understand that the hard work has not truly started yet."

So how does a student-athlete get the right type of attention at a large college showcase event? As discussed before, it is essential to initiate emails to college coaches a few weeks prior to the event to let them know of your interest in the school and provide the competition schedule, locations, jersey colors and numbers, and academic information.

R. J. Enga, Assistant Hockey Coach at NCAA Division I Colorado College, states, "I would say I get anywhere from 25 to 40 emails per week from prospective student-athletes normally. These emails increase a lot in volume prior to big tournaments and showcases.

We use these showcases a lot to evaluate, as they only count as one viewing for the weekend. It gives us a chance to get a better read on a player's ability, attitude, and character over the course of multiple games versus just one. The level of the showcase itself must be taken into consideration, so that we know the overall level is high enough to get an accurate read on this player."

During the Event
Expect Limited Contact with College Coaches.

Most college coaches will *not* be looking to interact with the student-athletes or their parents at the event. Every sport, college division, graduation year, and the showcase itself has different rules for contact with the student-athletes during the event. (These rules can be found on the governing body websites.) Do not assume that just because a coach is at the event that they may speak with potential recruits or their parents. In some sports and at certain levels, college coaches may only have a polite greeting for prospective student-athletes and their families at these events.

Let the college coach dictate the amount of interaction they can and want to engage in. Sometimes they want to speak to the recruit's club coach. Some other coaches will be looking for player profile résumés for the team from a team manager. It is recommended that a team book be compiled by a team manager with basic contact information, headshot pictures with jersey numbers, and individual academic and athletic information. These booklets should be handed out to the college coaches attending the competition by a team manager. While some sports have online profiles available, it is preferable to have these on hand for the coaches.

LET THE COLLEGE COACH DICTATE THE AMOUNT OF INTERACTION THEY CAN AND WANT TO ENGAGE IN.

Some levels and sports allow coaches to speak with the student-athlete immediately after a competition depending on the graduation year. Coaches may also need to move to the next competition, and getting caught up in unsolicited conversations with parents or student-athletes may not be desirable at that time. The college coaches are trying to make the most efficient use of their time at an event. Do not assume if a coach leaves the competition site that they are not interested; they may simply have seen what they need to and are moving on to evaluate another prospective student-athlete. They will communicate later if they are interested in a student-athlete, depending on the rules and regulations of their governing body.

Capitalize on Unique Qualities.

As mentioned regarding videos, the same is true for live events. Choose something visually that makes you stand out and keep it consistent. For example, if the student-athlete typically wears a braid in their hair, orange cleats, or a blue sweat band, let the college coaches know this in the initial emails so they can identify an athlete quickly beyond jersey number or positions. In some sports, jersey numbers can change throughout the season, so it is easier to let coaches know other characteristics in order for them to quickly identify the student-athlete.

Be Coachable.

You are ready for the competition to start and your coach is going over some last-minute reminders. You are looking in the stands to see if your girlfriend/boyfriend is there yet. You are tying your shoes or taking off your warm-up pants. You are talking to your favorite teammate to pep them up for the game.

Each of these behaviors demonstrates a lack of desire to listen to the coach and then implement instructions. Look directly at the coach, and fully concentrate on the instructions. Remember, college coaches want coachable student-athletes and can pick from hundreds of athletes at these events. Positive body language is critical during these events, especially after a bad play. Do not demonstrate behaviors on the sidelines that would lead them to question your coachability. No matter the score, coaches are looking for competitors. They evaluate *every* aspect that will translate into how you will act on their team.

POSITIVE BODY LANGUAGE IS CRITICAL DURING THESE EVENTS, ESPECIALLY AFTER A BAD PLAY.

Respect Your Parents.

Seeing a talented player walk over to their parent after a tough game and behave poorly can supersede any great notes written in the column next to that name. Saying you are too tired to carry your bag and throwing it toward your parents to carry may not seem like a big deal, but coaches see it differently.

When asked, "What turns you off instantly when you are watching a recruit play?" seven coaches cautioned basically the same thing: "I hate it when they complain about the color of Gatorade their parent is kindly handing them after a game!"

Obviously, it's a small problem, but it indicates a bigger one to coaches: Entitlement. When you have a team of 12–85 student-athletes (depending on the sport) and the coach or athletic trainer brings over a cooler full of a sports drink that isn't your favorite type, they don't want to hear whining. And if you whine and complain to your parents, you are likely to do the same to your coaches. No coach wants that and will simply move on.

Demonstrate Good Character.

Make sure the way you are communicating to your teammates before, during, and after competition demonstrates maturity and positive interactions to solve adversity. Coaches are looking for future leaders. If the student-athlete (or parent) is constantly complaining to the officials or criticizing team members or coach's decisions, the college coaches will gladly move on to the next field or court. More college scholarship offers have been lost due to these factors than to the ability to play at the next level.

After the Event

Many student-athletes email a college coach after the event for follow-up, but it is essential to give coaches time to get caught up from traveling and evaluating hundreds of potential recruits. Kelly Bryan, Assistant Athletic Director and the Head Women's Soccer Coach at Kenyon College in Ohio, encourages student-athletes to be patient. "My absolute least favorite part of the recruiting process is emailing the recruits after a showcase. By the time I travel home and get back to work, I already have five emails from recruits asking why I haven't given them any feedback yet. Give me a few days, please!"

MARKETING TO CHRISTIAN COLLEGE COACHES

Families should consider some unique aspects as they research Christian colleges for their student-athlete specifically during the application process and campus visits. For many faith-based colleges, it is essential for student-athletes to offer information to coaches in their initial emails regarding their desire to be in a Christian environment.

Jody Martinez has spent 27 years coaching basketball and 18 years in athletic administration. He currently serves as the Head Women's Basketball Coach at Taylor University in Indiana. "You must have a spiritual statement of faith to attend. Our mission is to equip and develop future Christian leaders through our culture on campus and through our individual sports. We are looking for recruits that have a faith background and know that their main priority in life is their personal relationship with Jesus Christ. We don't want other things to become 'idols' or 'passions' that their walk in Christ suffers."

Brad McCarty, Associate Athletic Director and the Head Men's Soccer Coach at Messiah College, looks for student-athletes who "care about their Christian faith, have a growth mindset, and strong work ethic. On the field, we want them to have a great soccer IQ and know that they will be a positional fit into our 4-3-3 system."

Tim Hays won a national championship in women's basketball in the National Christian Colleges Association of America (NCCAA) in NCAA DII and now serves as the Head Women's Coach at Southeastern University in the NAIA. He encourages recruits to describe in their initial emails "an understanding that ministry and excellence are one and the same. Striving to use every gift fully and practically in the day-to-day process of becoming a finished product that honors the Lord. Be clear in illustrating why a Christian university is a fit outside of just the sport."

Jerry Schemmel offers a unique perspective as the Radio Announcer for the Colorado Rockies who worked for eight years as a college baseball coach at both secular and Christian universities. "Recruits should describe their desire to experience the incredibly valuable aspects of a Christian education outside of athletics. Like developing or strengthening a student athlete's walk with Christ, bonding with other students over spiritual matters rather than social and athletic, experiencing a more intimate setting in the classroom and hopefully having coaches that will love and strengthen you in more places than just the field."

He continues, "For the sport of baseball, I often told recruits that the odds were stacked against them in terms of playing professionally. We would do all we could to give them that opportunity, but it was a long shot most of the time. Therefore, the education should be more important than athletics. Most kids who contacted me were simply looking for a place to play baseball and not necessarily interested in a Christian college. I would recommend that anyone interested in a Christian school be very frank and open about why."

To encourage this direct communication, include the following in initial emails to coaches at Christian colleges:

1. **The student-athlete's desire to grow in their faith life and a commitment to the lifestyle choices of the college.**

   The student-athlete needs to demonstrate their desire to be in a Christian environment versus the parent's desire for the student-athlete in their local church. This should also include a statement of when the student-athlete accepted Christ, their vision for sports ministry, and the calling God has placed on their life.

2. **Active participation by the student-athlete (not just the family's) involvement in a local church.**

3. **Any involvement and leadership roles in youth groups, worship teams, retreats, or faith-based organizations** (such as Fellowship of Christian Athletes [FCA], Young Life, etc.)

4. **Serving in the local community, including leading a Bible study, helping with Vacation Bible School, Habitat for Humanity, or Big Brothers/Big Sisters.**

5. **Describe any experiences in serving on domestic and international mission trips.**

6. **References who have known the student-athlete beyond the classroom well for two or more years and who can speak about their character and spiritual walk.**

A youth group leader, pastor, FCA adviser, worship leader, or someone similar should be able to speak about the student-athlete's lifestyle choices of avoiding partying, serving in the community, and what they could contribute to a team environment.

INTERNATIONAL STUDENT-ATHLETE CONSIDERATIONS

International students wanting to study in the United States need to understand the college recruiting process is a bit more complicated due to the need for international government documents to be processed in order for them to qualify for student visas to enter the country. Every country of origin for the student and each specific college has a different set of procedures, so it is key to start early in the student's high school career.

1. **International student-athletes need to research and contact coaches early and should not wait until their senior year to start the process.** Due to the amount of paperwork and timelines to process international applications, it is essential for an international student-athlete to decide which college is the best fit for them academically, athletically, socially, and especially, financially, as early as possible.

Kelly Rider, the Head Women's Hockey Coach and Senior Women's Administrator at Northland College, states, "I recruit Canadian student-athletes all the time and occasionally some from Europe. I advise them to be proactive and take initiative to reach out to coaches and send videos. Ask coaches the right questions about how internationals are treated throughout the admissions process as each school can be slightly different."

2. **International student-athletes need to be granted a student visa.** In order to enter the United States, a student-athlete needs to apply and be accepted to a university, and have been granted a student visa (called an I-20) by the Student and Exchange Program. A student visa is a travel document that is received by a US consulate or embassy before the student enters the United States. A student's status is what that person must maintain after they are granted entrance into the United States. There are a lot of important steps to this process, and I highly recommend researching more information at studyinthestates.dhs.gov/faq.

3. **For non-native speakers, they should take the Test of English as a Foreign Language (TOEFL) to measure their English language skills, as needed for admissions to the college.** Visit www.ets.org/toefl for more information.

4. **Register and send official (English-translated) transcripts and SAT scores to both the college and the Eligibility Centers.** Visit www.collegeboard.org for more information.

5. **Answer all questions related to amateurism and provide any specifically requested documentation to the Eligibility Center.** Visit www.ncaa.org and www.naia.org for more information.

CHAPTER 5

ROLES OF THE STUDENT-ATHLETE, PARENTS, COACHES, AND HIGH SCHOOL PERSONNEL

STUDENT-ATHLETE'S ROLE

Student-athletes should be fully engaged in the recruiting process. They should not be waiting on a parent, coach, or high school staff to let colleges know that they are interested in being evaluated. Many families sit back and expect someone to help the student-athlete "get seen". Mark Friese, Principal of Stonington High School in Connecticut, played and coached basketball in high school. He believes, "The student-athlete should be the primary mover in the process."

While coaches, principals, school counselors, and athletic directors will be a great support system during the recruiting process, the support system should *not* be expected to do the work the student-athlete needs to be doing. Coaches may eventually want to speak with all these people to get a better understanding of the overall student-athlete, but college coaches reiterated again and again during the interviews that they want the initial contact to come from the student-athlete.

THE SUPPORT SYSTEM SHOULD *NOT* BE EXPECTED TO DO THE WORK THE STUDENT-ATHLETE NEEDS TO BE DOING.

It is also essential that student-athletes are doing everything they can to excel. Brent Tisdale, Principal of Heard High School in Atlanta, Georgia, believes student-athletes need to "take care of business in the classroom, push themselves in the weight room, and keep out of trouble on social media."

PARENT'S ROLE

Adam Ritchie is the Technical Director at Southwest Virginia Rush Soccer Club and the Men's Head Coach at New River Community College. He has helped in the recruiting process of hundreds of athletes while previously serving as a high school head coach for 12 years and Director of Coaching for 15 years. "Parents should proofread what the player is sending to colleges. They should also make sure that their child is following up with colleges even if they do not want to play at a school. Too many times players just ignore coaches from schools they do not want to play for early on. Little do they know that the landscape of college coaching changes quickly and you do not know if the coach you just ignored ends up at a school you want to attend."

Most parents of high school student-athletes want their child to receive an athletic scholarship to continue their sport in college. The recruiting process can be completely daunting to the student-athlete amid their practice schedule, ACT/SAT test prep, and keeping up with their classes. It becomes so overwhelming that many parents try to help their young athletes by emailing or calling a college coach, using the excuse their child is too busy.

Dr. David Fleming, Faculty Member and Associate Dean at Clemson University, has 25 years of experience in high school and higher education, and has four children who all received DI athletic scholarship offers. "A student athlete that demonstrates the independence to navigate the recruiting and college selection process without a helicopter parent pulling the strings is a much better bet to be successful on their own when they matriculate .. Rather, the parents should clearly stay in the background and demonstrate that their child will be successful without their constant presence and feedback."

Most college coaches and athletic directors revealed that a parent making the Initial contact is completely frowned upon for the following reasons:

1. **It appears the parent wants their child to continue in their sport more than the child does.**

To make matters worse, the parent will often say, "Well, my child is shy and doesn't know what to say to a coach." College coaches want to interact with the student-athlete directly, since they could be in their program for the next four years.

Rex Bowman, Athletic Director at Kings Ridge Christian School in Alpharetta, Georgia, suggests, "If your child is not comfortable talking to people they don't know, make them do phone conversations for a month with a telemarketer or ordering a pizza."

2. It sends a warning signal that the parent may be a "helicopter" parent.

College coaches want parents to be huge cheerleaders for their son or daughter, but not to hover over every aspect of the college athletic program. There is nothing worse than a potential recruit sitting in a coach's office and the parents asking a ton of questions while the child sits there with little to say. This "handholding" behavior by the parent does not benefit the student-athlete at all long term. The coaching staff wants to see the athlete demonstrate leadership skills.

3. It signals that the student is likely lazy, struggles with time management, and/or is not mature enough to engage in adult conversations.

Being a college student-athlete requires a great deal of discipline and time management skills. The recruiting process often reveals a student's readiness to balance the demands they will experience at the next level. When a parent writes an email saying their child is just way too busy, most university personnel view this as the student's major lack of maturity and inability to prioritize. It is imperative that students take the initiative in the interactions!

Most parents are just looking for ways to help their child and support the coaches, teams, and officials in positive ways. So, what can parents do to score points with college coaches?

Chad Metzler is the Executive Director of Lake Norman Soccer Club in North Carolina and has placed hundreds of his athletes at colleges at all levels and in all areas of the country. He has served as a head coach for the club and has been educating families on the college recruiting process for two decades. "I encourage parents to be less involved with communicating with the schools, but the parents should be more involved in helping their teen understand the process as most teens are not equipped to pick a school."

He continues, "Generally, when I ask a freshman in high school to give me a list of five schools they are interested in, they will be large top Division I schools because they have not heard of anything else. Parents need to help drive the process by visiting colleges and take an active role early on. If you can figure out a bit about what they want regarding size, location, major, and other social factors that can help generate 15 similar schools. Parents need to be more proactive to help kids figure out what's out there."

1. **Take an active approach in the recruiting process but not the lead in communicating with college coaches.**

While it is important for the student-athlete to initiate contact with the college coach, a parent can help the student-athlete understand what is important in choosing a college besides athletics (i.e., location, academic opportunities, college size, career opportunities, etc.). A parent can help them wade through the college brochures and camp invites to create a spreadsheet of information comparing the colleges and universities. They also can help by proofreading emails.

2. **Proactively help the student-athlete value academics early.**

Many student-athletes do not think freshmen or sophomore grades matter. Yet, they can make a huge impact in the long run. Also, it's important to schedule ACT/SAT tests late sophomore or early junior year to allow time to retake the tests if the first score isn't ideal.

3. Be realistic and help the student-athlete be open to opportunities.

Depending on the sport, NCAA statistics show that only about three percent to ten percent of high school student-athletes receive athletic scholarships. This number can vary across sports and other levels such as the NAIA and NJCAA, but it is rarely a double-digit percentage.

Many young athletes only choose to play in college because their parents pushed them into it. These athletes often lack motivation and are just "going through the motions". Many coaches believe this happens because the parents often just assume their child wanted to continue to play, without even asking. Parents need to support their student-athlete by asking if they really want to commit to playing at the next level.

4. Be aware that a parent's behavior on the sidelines can impact a college coach's decision.

Many college coaches interviewed discussed how often the parent of a prospective student athlete deterred them from recruiting or offering a scholarship to a highly talented athlete.

HIGH SCHOOL COUNSELOR'S ROLE

Trying to meet the academic, athletic, and social needs of a single student-athlete can be challenging enough, but imagine trying to help hundreds of students. When it comes to academic guidance, the American School Counselor Association recommends a ratio of one school counselor for every 250 students. Unfortunately, in many school districts across the country, a school counselor may have more than 400 in their caseload. So how can they possibly serve so many students' academic, emotional, and intellectual needs, let alone prepare them for college? School counselors can help student-athletes start planning for college by doing the following:

1. Engaging in strategic planning.

During the student-athlete's freshman and sophomore years, school counselors can help in planning the right core courses needed for eligibility at all levels. Do not assume that because a student-athlete is on track to graduate, they will be automatically eligible for intercollegiate athletics. Students with 4.0+ GPAs can be deemed ineligible because they did not take the required coursework in high school. Since there are variances across the governing bodies of the NCAA, NAIA, and NJCAA, counselors need to use the NCAA DI and DII Guides as they help plan their student-athletes' schedules.

2. Reminding student athletes that grades matter.

Many families think college coaches can get a talented kid into a college just based on their athletic ability and by "pulling a few strings". While this practice happened a lot 20 to 30 years ago, it is very rare today. Eligibility is still regulated by the governing body and not by the individual college.

If a college coach invites a student-athlete to be a part of their program, they do not want to deal with academic issues. School counselors should guide and direct student-athletes early in high school regarding the importance of their GPA in core courses and the need to take academics seriously. College coaches do not want to have to worry about student-athletes being accepted into the college or about eligibility. They have thousands of recruits to choose from, so they look for the best overall student-athlete.

3. College Tests

School counselors should encourage student-athletes to take their first ACT and/or SAT tests as early as the end of sophomore year or the fall of junior year (if they have had the necessary coursework, especially for math). They should advise taking each test multiple times, as most colleges now "super score" (taking the best subscores from various tests to make the best possible combined score) for determining college acceptance and merit scholarships.

4. "The Broken Leg Test"

It is imperative that the school counselors help student-athletes think through academic majors, size of the college, distance from home, social setting, city versus rural campus, affordability, and overall internship and career opportunities. They should help determine what would be a great fit across the board and not just focus on athletic scholarship amounts.

School counselors should also encourage the student-athlete to make unofficial visits to local colleges during their freshman and sophomore years to get a baseline perspective. Too often families wait until the student-athlete's junior or senior year to start looking at colleges. For the student-athlete, this is often too late, and the college coaches have already chosen their recruiting class.

5. Encouraging student-athletes to properly market themselves.

School counselors can help student-athletes understand the importance of properly marketing themselves to college coaches beyond athletics. They should encourage student-athletes to be involved in community service and other extracurriculars beyond their sport. They also should help in the process of having transcripts sent to the colleges of interest.

CLUB COACH OR HIGH SCHOOL STAFF'S ROLE

Some families expect that the high school/club coach or athletic director will generate interest from college coaches for student-athletes to be identified as a potential recruit. This should not be the expectation, however, especially since most college coaches want initially to hear of the interest in a school directly from the student-athlete. High school and club coaches can make a follow-up call or email to the colleges to endorse the talent and character of a prospective student-athlete. It is important to note that in some sports and at some levels, the depth of the conversation may be a bit restricted by the governing body for that college.

It is also essential for high school or club coaches to be completely objective in their evaluations, even though they may want to really help their player attend a specific college or receive an athletic scholarship offer. They need to help families maintain perspective and focus on showing character, developing a strong work ethic, being a good teammate, and placing academics in the forefront.

Greg Byrne, Director of Athletics at the University of Alabama, encourages high school and club coaches to "remember to coach the student-athlete from a genuine approach. Mentor and support them and hold young people accountable. Make sure they are doing the right things academically, socially, and athletically."

Patrick Crowdis, Principal of Spearville Junior and Senior High School in Kansas, has former student-athletes who went on to play NCAA Division I football and basketball, and then play in the NFL and the NBA. "The high school coach should be offering the objective view and offering a better understanding to where the athlete would be more suited versus focusing on only helping kids be a Division I recruit."

Jody Martinez, the Head Women's Basketball Coach at Taylor University in Indiana, has more than 28 years in coaching. "My biggest pet peeve is the AAU (club) and high school coaches who overpromote their players that are not very good and not Division I. There have been times I flat out told coaches that their credibility is on the line when they promote a player and the evaluation from us (college coaches) doesn't match up. Just because a player might be your best player, doesn't mean that they are college skill material."

University of Florida Athletic Director Scott Stricklin agrees, "Make it about the kids—not about their ego."

Similar to the coaches, it should not be the athletic director's role to initially market the student-athlete to the college coaches. The high school athletic director should also take a supportive role in the process for the student-athlete and provide information to colleges as needed. However, athletic directors also need to be responsible for making sure that all student-athletes, their parents, and coaches are being educated to fully understand how the college recruiting process works for specific sports by graduation year and within specific governing bodies.

John Cavell, a retired high school principal and referee/umpire for more than a decade in multiple sports throughout the Southeast, says, "Every sports season, we had a meeting with all the parents to address and inform them about the recruiting process."

It is essential that recruiting education programs take place every year in high schools and club programs to help equip families to take the right steps in marketing student-athletes to colleges. Athletic programs and booster clubs should budget for the educational programs as it is an essential part of the process. For information on educational webinars, live seminars, blogs, and Facebook groups for parents and coaches, visit www.rlopezcoaching.com or email info@lookingforafullride.com.

CHAPTER 6

BEYOND THE X'S AND O'S: WHAT COACHES WANT

A few years ago, I received an email and video link from a talented student-athlete documenting the number of goals she had scored for both her high school and club soccer travel teams. She had a 3.5 GPA, high ACT scores, was driven toward a medical career, and had expressed serious interest in both our academic and athletic program. We were very interested in her as we knew she would create the offensive threat our team needed for that recruiting class.

She was playing in an upcoming college showcase tournament, so we made sure my assistant and I could both attend her game. We watched warm-ups and about 30 minutes of the first half. She demonstrated even more skill as an offensive threat than we had seen on her film. She scored a beautiful goal from about 30 yards out. However, when the opposing team tied the game, she kept screaming at the referee saying the goal was offsides. (It wasn't.) When the other team then went up two to one, she yelled at her teammate from across the field about a mistake that led to the goal. As the opposing team stretched the lead to three to one (after her own mark scored), she asked the coach to take her out of the game saying, "No one is trying to help us win!" We picked up our recruiting chairs and walked away, knowing we had seen all we needed to see.

When college coaches are on the sidelines evaluating a potential recruit, they are observing *every* aspect of the athlete. Sure, every coach wants a talented athlete to help their team win. But coaches want to see how a student-athlete handles the roller coaster of emotions involved in playing a college sport. They want to know how student-athletes will respond to adversity. After their opposition scores on them, what is their response? Is it to step up to the challenge by taking ownership to solve problems, or are they blaming their teammates, the referees, or coaches for their team's not-so-stellar performance? What are they saying on social media after these difficult times?

As we picked up our chairs that day, my assistant and I discussed how we were looking to enhance our team cohesion, not disrupt our positive team culture. It's rather funny how the story panned out as the student-athlete ended up attending a conference rival and started as a freshman. Early in the season we went to scout that opponent, and she made a huge impact in scoring goals, but behaved exactly in the same manner we witnessed at that college showcase.

By the end of the year, she was not in the starting lineup. I saw her warm-up against us, but she was never put in. I later asked the opposing coach why she did not play, guessing she was injured or sick. The coach just shook his head saying, "I should have watched her live. I only watched her film. She has caused nothing but disruptions in our team chemistry this entire year and hurt our efforts to win games. Most of the players don't want her here even though they know she scores gouls."

STEP UP TO THE CHALLENGE BY TAKING OWNERSHIP TO SOLVE PROBLEMS.

Remember this story when a coach wants to see a student-athlete play live, even after they have viewed a great video showcasing their abilities. (Be cautious of any program that only uses videotape to assess potential recruits!)

NECESSARY INTANGIBLES

As mentioned earlier, mature student-athletes make a college coach's job easier. They want teenagers who are responsible, independent, and dependable to represent their colleges in the best way possible (and not end up in the media for making poor choices).

Scott Stricklin, University of Florida Athletic Director, believes, "Leadership is in short supply. We need young people to be good leaders, and this is often the hardest to identify during the recruiting process. It is a valued trait, along with the integrity and character piece, to do the right thing. My advice is to make good grades, be a good teammate, and establish a strong work ethic academically and athletically. Develop good habits [in high school] to be able to battle through adversity in college."

In interview after interview, college coaches and athletic directors reiterated their desire to recruit student-athletes possessing these intangibles:

1. A Team-First Mentality

Frank Mateus is a former DI college head coach and currently the Director of Coaching with the Rockford Raptors Club. He also serves as the College Advisory Program Director for high school student-athletes who look to continue playing in college. He explains, "College coaches are evaluating all aspects of a recruit. They want to see how they impact other players around them. Are they acting as a leader when their team faces adversity? Do they have the ability to make other players better?"

In 1998, Jim Thompson founded the Positive Coaching Alliance (PCA), a nonprofit movement to make youth sports a development zone, which promotes "Better Athletes, Better People". In his book, *Becoming A Triple-Impact Competitor*, Thompson emphasizes, "Do you look to shine the spotlight on your teammates to give them credit for their contributions rather than trying to get maximum credit for yourself?"

Ken Kavanagh is the Director of Athletics at DI Florida Gulf Coast University and formerly also held that position at DI Bradley University in Illinois. He shares, "Colleges want individuals who are self-starters, team oriented, and all-around leaders who value the name on the front of their proverbial jerseys more than their own names on the back and who appreciate the bigger picture of what athletics should be about including: Enjoying your sport at highest level and generating life long memories with your teammates!"

College coaches want leaders who mentor and help develop future leaders, not just develop themselves. Author, speaker, and leadership expert John Maxwell observes, "A leader's lasting value is measured by succession." They want student-athletes who leave a lasting positive legacy after they graduate.

2. Ability to Demonstrate Respect and Integrity

"It is imperative that a potential recruit's character is that which someone would be willing to invest hundreds of thousands of dollars in scholarships and resources into," advised Joshua Rebholz, the Senior Associate Athletic Director at UCLA for the past 14 years.

College coaches want to see that a potential recruit can demonstrate respect for not only their own parents and coaches but also their opponents and the officials. They want student-athletes who will represent the college well and value everyone they come in contact with daily while wearing the team uniform.

One great principle related to respect on teams comes from an unlikely source for a sports book: Lee Cockerell, the former Executive VP of Operations at Walt Disney World Resorts who spent more than 40 years in the hospitality industry. Lee is one of the public faces of the Disney Institute, which focuses on leadership development and on building teams.

In his book, *Creating Magic,* he discusses a Disney Institute concept of RAVE (Respect, Appreciate, and Value Everyone). He believes this idea applies to any team, whether in business or sports. Throughout the interviews of the 65 college coaches and athletic directors for this book, these principles were regularly emphasized as determining factors in deciding between recruits. Most college coaches are not afraid to cross a recruit off their list if they do not demonstrate the character and maturity needed for college athletics.

Coach Kevin Lubbers was honored as the NCCAA Men's Basketball Coach of the Year in 2017 while coaching at Colorado Christian University and now he works with high school student-athletes as the Athletic Director at Wheaton Academy in Illinois. He says, "We always look for feedback from the janitor, cafeteria worker, or principal at the high school. Do they represent themselves well to everyone around them? Are they respectful and authentic? Are they respectful to their coaches, teammates, and officials?"

College and professional coaches want athletes who make good choices away from their coaches. Former NFL coach Tony Dungy emphasizes the importance of having integrity and engaging in good decision-making away from coaches. In his book, *Uncommon: Finding Your Path to Significance,* Dungy emphasizes, "Much of my work is dependent upon things that my players and coaches do when no one is watching them. I suppose I could watch as much as possible, but I don't like micromanaging . . . If I'm going to help those around me grow as people, they are going to have to take responsibility for what they do when I'm not watching."

3. Capability to Develop and Sacrifice Daily

College coaches want athletes who try every day to develop themselves and those around them. They want to know if potential recruits are willing to commit to making the sacrifices needed to be a high-level athlete such as getting rest and good nutrition, staying focused in academics, participating in community service, participating in injury prevention and weight training programs, and growing as a leader.

Tami Matheny is a Mental Game Coach and author of *The Confident Athlete.* She has worked with numerous high school and college sports teams across the United States to help them build confidence, team chemistry, and deal with mental setbacks. One guiding principle she uses in her work with student-athletes is a Japanese business term called *kaizen,* meaning continuous improvement.

In the book *Kaizen, the Key to Japan's Competitive Success,* author Masaaki Imai emphasizes, "Kaizen means ongoing improvement involving everyone." Would others who regularly interact with the student-athlete describe him or her as having this attribute? Be aware that college coaches may ask anyone that knows a student-athlete about their daily habits. They may solicit opinions from an opposing coach, an English teacher, a minister, a school secretary, or even an official.

What would a high school or club coach say about this student-athlete to a coach? Would they say they just "go through the motions", or do they have an innate desire to improve in every aspect of their lives? Coaches want intrinsically motivated student-athletes.

In his book *The Power of Positive Leadership,* Jon Gordon describes the *one percent rule.* "The rule says to give one percent more time, energy, effort, focus, and care today than you gave yesterday. Each day give more than you did the day before. Obviously, you can't calculate one percent, but you can push yourself more today than you did yesterday. You can tune out distractions and focus even more on what matters most." Gordon's *one percent rule* applies to the types of student-athletes college coaches look for daily.

4. Ability to Be Coachable and Resilient

As a teen, one of my favorite coaches was named Gordy Poluyanskis. He always pushed me to be better and taught me the ways to fix mistakes on the field. He was super patient with me because he wanted to help me to play in college. To say the least, I wasn't always overwhelmingly excited to hear him correct me. And I am ashamed to say I would often give him a bit of attitude when he tried to help me, especially during practice. Luckily, when college coaches were attending games, I was not disrespectful, or I never would have been recruited to play in college.

College coaches want athletes who are receptive to feedback from their coaches, especially when facing adversity. They want student-athletes who have resiliency. They want positive and hard-working athletes, not those who are frozen in negativity as they face a difficult situation.

In John Maxwell's book *Sometimes You Win, Sometimes You Learn*, he suggests that everyone responds to challenging circumstances in one of three ways: Everyone is like an egg, a carrot, or a coffee bean. In boiling water, an egg hardens, and a carrot softens. A coffee bean becomes a great cup of coffee when it is in boiling water. As a student-athlete, college coaches want to see potential recruits look at adversity as an opportunity to become something better, not to drag others down. Become a great cup of coffee!

THEY WANT STUDENT-ATHLETES WHO HAVE RESILIENCY. THEY WANT POSITIVE AND HARD-WORKING ATHLETES.

In his *Wall Street Journal* bestseller *The Energy Bus,* Jon Gordon writes, "Your success and life are so important that you must surround yourself with a positive support team . . . I call the people who drain your energy, *Energy Vampires,* and they will suck the life out of you and your goals and vision if you let them."

When your team is facing a lot of uphill battles, whether from a lot of injuries to your members, poor officiating, or lopsided competition, it is important that you do not become an *Energy Vampire*. College coaches watch your body language, the tone of your voice, and the overall energy you project when facing a difficult situation; they want players who handle challenges with maturity, class, and dignity.

5. Willingness to Give Back to the Community

College coaches want student-athletes who look beyond themselves and serve their community. They want young adults who can see the bigger picture and the platform that sports can often provide to improve another person's life.

Tim Tebow is a favorite of many, and not just because of his outstanding talent in football and now minor league baseball. It's because he is an amazing athlete who inspires others around him and uses sports as a platform to make the world a better place. His Christian faith is lived out in his work building hospitals overseas and creating prom nights for high school kids with special needs.

In his book, *Shaken: Discovering Your True Identity in the Midst of Life's Storm,* he describes his calling, "I want to bring faith, hope, and love to those needing a brighter day in their darkest hour of need. I want to fight for those who could not fight for themselves."

Athletic programs want to know what a student-athlete is doing to serve others and cast a brighter vision for the world. College coaches want well-rounded athletes and caring individuals. Most college teams participate in various community philanthropy events and would love student-athletes who will take the lead to help the community!

CHAPTER 7

PLANNING A
CAMPUS VISIT

M any families learn the most about a college by making a campus visit. Susan Peal has served as NCAA Director of Governance of the National Letter of Intent (NLI) program for the past 29 years. She states, "One of the biggest mistakes is a prospective student-athlete who does not take an official or unofficial visit before they sign an NLI. You cannot make such an important life decision without visiting campus and talking to as many people as possible about their experiences at that institution."

Scott Myers, a former Director of Admissions, has also been a college track and field coach for ten years. "It is never too early to start looking at schools. There are a variety of ways to do this—visit a college nearby to see a game or even a musical performance so you can enhance your exposure to college life.

"Eat in the dining hall, and you will see students and maybe some faculty members interacting with students. You'll see the social dynamics. Is it all fraternity and sorority intermingling? Plus, you must like the food!"

It is also important to keep perspective while meeting with Admissions and doing a campus tour. Bill Bufton, College Recruiting Coordinator for Student-Athletes at Valor Christian High School, warns, "Kids can be enamored by facilities. Remember, they are 'wooing' you. You can easily be distracted. It's important to focus on the culture of the team and the degrees that they offer. Embarrassingly, many kids focus on uniform brand name. You need to look past all of that and focus on the long-term benefits."

UNOFFICIAL VISITS

Those seriously interested in pursuing a sport in college should visit several college campuses early in high school to compare campus facilities, gain a better understanding of the admissions process, meet with various faculty in a potential academic major(s), and see up-close the demands of being a college student. An unofficial visit to a college by a prospective student-athlete is made at the prospective student-athlete's own expense.

Some colleges only do unofficial visits. Stevan Hernandez is the Head Men's Soccer Coach at St. Andrew's University, an NAIA college in North Carolina. He says, "All we do are unofficial visits. I believe if you are truly interested in us, then we hope that you would make a financial commitment to come visit."

There are some restrictions for some sports in terms of *timing* for unofficial visits during high school, but typically a student-athlete can do an unlimited number of unofficial visits. This information can be found on the websites of the governing bodies in the glossary.

What to Take on an Unofficial Visit

Spend a lot of time on the college website *prior to* a visit to get familiar with the college and prepare a list of questions to ask Admissions, current students, faculty, and athletic staff. Prior to visiting a campus, check with Admissions about parking locations. Print a campus map from the college website.

Also, take a copy of recent transcripts, test scores, a one-page player profile/résumé that includes Eligibility Center ID numbers, letters of recommendation, and other supporting materials.

Costs and Compensation

Colleges are very limited in what expenses and activities they are allowed to provide for during an unofficial campus visit depending on the sport and graduation year. They may be able to transport a student-athlete to view practice facilities and their home competition facilities. They may pick up one meal in the on-campus dining facility or at a local restaurant for the prospective student-athlete and relatives/legal guardians. However, it is best not to expect the college to cover any expenses.

Staying Overnight in the Residence Halls

It is important to ask about lodging when setting up the unofficial visit. Do not wait until the day of the visit. In most cases, the prospective student-athlete may stay in an enrolled student-athlete's dorm if they pay the going rate for regular (non-athletic) prospective students for such lodging. At most colleges, this is complimentary, but some will charge. Again, this may or may not be permitted based on sport, graduation year, and level of competition.

What to Expect

Most colleges will accommodate taking a campus tour, meeting with Admissions and Financial Aid, touring residence halls, eating in the dining facilities, and meeting with faculty in a desired academic major(s). Basically, the student-athlete can do anything any other prospective student would do in evaluating a college.

Meeting with the Coaching Staff

It depends on the sport, graduation year, and level of competition. Do not assume that a coach can or has time to meet with you, especially on competition days if the meeting is not prearranged. **College coaches do NOT like it when a student-athlete just shows up unannounced in their office.**

College coaches receive hundreds of emails from recruits each month. They want to refresh their memory of who you are in terms of talent, academics, and your social media presence prior to a meeting with you. **Instead, try to arrange a meeting through Admissions a week or two before the visit (if allowed based on the sport, graduation year, and level of competition).**

It is also imperative to understand that on competition days, they may not have a lot of free time to spend with you, no matter how far you traveled or how much they love you as a recruit. The day of a game is one of the busiest days for a coach, especially the head coach. There is so much going on behind the scenes, from giving media interviews, dealing with injuries, participating in coaching staff meetings, and of course, interacting with their current players, administrators, and officials. It is better to go visit the day before a competition to have a better chance of meeting with some of the coaching staff.

Complimentary Tickets

Depending on the sport, graduation year, and level of competition it's possible to receive some complimentary admissions during an unofficial visit. These are not typically physical tickets; instead, the coaches will put names on a pass list at a specific ticket gate. At some levels of the NCAA and NAIA, there are complimentary admissions available for a prospective student-athlete and their parents. For nontraditional families (stepparents, etc.), two more complimentary tickets may be offered. Again, do not assume complimentary tickets will be offered as there are many rules regarding this at various levels.

Playing with the Team

Tryouts are not allowed at some levels, depending on the sport. There are stipulations for doing tryouts during certain periods of the school year. Most programs will also require you to have a copy of a recent physical for a sport, and sometimes this needs to include a sickle-cell anemia test.

Do not assume you are or are not doing a tryout. Ask the coaches if they want you to do this prior to traveling to the school. In some sports, you can attend an Identification (ID) Camp, which would allow you to pay to participate in a camp on campus at various times during the year.

Setting up an Unofficial Visit

It is best to work through Admissions, especially if the college coach cannot directly contact the student-athlete due to recruiting regulations. If regulations prevent direct contact, ask a high school/ club coach to help with communication (again, not all sports and levels permit this so research the current rules for the governing body). However, in some sports (depending on your graduation year), this may not be permissible.

What Should Families Wear on a Campus Visit?

Comfortable walking shoes should be a priority, as there will typically be a lot of walking. Wear something nicer than just athletic clothes or jeans. You want to make a good first impression, but you do not have to be in a business suit. Think "business casual"; a nice button-down shirt (tucked in) and dress pants for men, and a casual skirt or dress pants and nice blouse or sweater for women. It is also smart to dress in layers, in case campus buildings are too hot or too cold.

OFFICIAL VISITS

DO NOT ASSUME YOU ARE GOING TO BE INVITED FOR AN OFFICIAL VISIT JUST BECAUSE A SCHOOL IS RECRUITING YOU.

While three percent to ten percent of high school student-athletes get an opportunity to play at the next level, depending on the sport, not all of them are offered an athletic scholarship. Even fewer are offered an opportunity to do an official campus visit on the school's dime.

Most college coaches, admissions staff, and faculty agree that visiting a college campus can be extremely valuable, especially early in high school. To help determine the right fit, visit multiple campuses that are much different from each other—big and small, city versus suburb, and with various levels of sports competition.

Do Not Expect to Be Offered an Official Visit

One NCAA Division I head coach (who asked to remain anonymous so he could speak bluntly) said, "One of my biggest pet peeves in the college recruiting process is that so many high school student-athletes, and especially their parents, have the impression that colleges have an unending amount of money in their recruiting budgets to fly kids in from all across the country on a whim when they may or may not be interested in our college."

He continued, "I appreciate the anonymity in this as I say this as kindly, yet as bluntly as I can . . . Our recruiting budgets are not like the SEC or ACC, even though we are DI. Here's the scenario families need to understand. If I can fly myself and my assistant to a college showcase or tournament and see 500 to 1,000 kids play in one weekend for the same cost of flying one student-athlete in to see our campus and entertain them, who *may or may not* commit to us... What would you do to be a good steward of the limited recruiting budget for our team? Some recruits think that just because they are a talented athlete, that they deserve an official visit."

He added, "Please let your readers know that they should see being offered an official visit as a privilege, not a right. *Do not ask for an official visit or athletic scholarship in your initial email!* You would never believe the number of kids who do this. It demonstrates a lack of knowledge of the process, realities of athletic department finances, and, worse, an attitude of entitlement, which coaches do not want on their teams. Most student-athletes should focus on unofficial visits and be gracious if they are offered an official visit."

Another DI athletic director echoed these thoughts (and also spoke on the condition of anonymity): "Student-athletes who are offered official visits should really be serious about the school being in their top three to five choices. Please do not use these official visits as a fun getaway for a weekend and act inappropriately while visiting the college. It will get around to other athletic programs as college sports is a tight-knit industry. Do not simply waste a coach's time and the school's finances by taking official visits of schools you have zero intention of attending. Some people think that this will 'drive their stock up' in terms of scholarship offers. It's simply not the way the system works."

John Cunningham, Deputy Athletic Director for Administration at the University of Minnesota, echoed the same thoughts, "Prospects taking official visits to schools they are not serious about is very frustrating. Don't waste the schools' time and money."

There are a lot of regulations regarding official visits, so the following simplifies some of the information by answering some frequently asked questions. The focus is on NCAA rules at the DI and DII levels which can often change so please consult the NCAA website for the most up-to-date legislation. Please note: NCAA DIII, NAIA, NCCAA, and NJCAA all have different rules when it comes to campus visits, so it is best to check with the governing body of the prospective college.

Who Pays for an Official Visit?

According to the NCAA website:

An official visit is any visit to a college or university campus by you and your parents that is paid for by the college. The college or university may pay all or some of the following expenses:

1. *Transportation to and from the college (for DI basketball and FBS football, this may include coach-class airfare for up to two people).*

2. *Room and meals (three per day) while you are visiting the college/university.*

3. *Reasonable entertainment expenses, including up to six complimentary admissions to a home athletics contest for Division I, or up to five complimentary admissions to a home athletics contest for Division II.*

What Needs to Be Done in Advance?

A prospective student-athlete cannot make an official visit until he or she

1. presents the institution with a current high school or college-preparatory school transcript (official or unofficial);

2. registers with the NCAA Eligibility Center; and

3. is placed on the institutional request list (IRL) by the college with the NCAA Eligibility Center.

Who Sets up an Official Visit?

The offer of an official visit comes from the college coach. Due to budgetary restrictions for many colleges, student-athletes should not have an expectation they will be offered an official visit just because they want to view the campus. Be honored If offered an official visit, but do not have the expectation or ask for an official visit. *This is not something student-athletes should just call and ask the coaching staff to do.*

How Many Official Visits Can I Make to a Specific Campus and Overall?

A member institution may finance only one visit to its campus for a prospective student-athlete, even if the student-athlete is exploring playing multiple sports. Some sports allow these visits to take place during the junior year of high school, while others only allow it at other times.

You may only be on campus for 48 hours or less as part of an official visit. It is important to note that you cannot do an official visit during any dead periods, which vary in timing by sport. Check the NCAA website for recruiting calendars that describe the specifics for each sport. Current legislation states a prospective student-athlete may take a maximum of five expense-paid visits to Division I institutions, with not more than one permitted to any single institution unless there are extenuating circumstances (in some sports). This restriction applies regardless of the number of sports in which the prospective student-athlete is involved.

What Should I Take?

Since the school will already have much of the required paperwork, ask the college coach if there is anything specific they would like you to bring. You should also have a list of questions to ask Admissions, current students, future teammates, faculty, and athletic staff.

Can I Stay Overnight in the Residence Halls?

A prospective student-athlete may stay in an enrolled student-athlete's residence hall. You will typically have a student-host who will supervise you while on campus. Remember that the college coach will ask for a report from that student-host about how you behaved socially during your visit. Make sure that you act maturely the entire time you are on the campus, ask a lot of questions, and avoid spending a lot of time on your phone!

Chad Metzler, the Executive Director for Lake Norman Soccer Club in North Carolina, states, "Overnight visits are super important. It's great when a kid can spend the night. They are on a bit of a trial. The coach will be asking the team what they thought. Lots of kids have been swayed completely one way or another after hanging out with the team."

What Should I Expect?

Most visits will include taking a campus tour, meeting with the Admissions and Financial Aid staff, touring residence halls, eating in the dining facilities, and speaking with academic representatives.

It varies on every college campus and depends if it's a weekday or weekend. The college coach will typically arrange all the details of an official visit, including attending a home competition and meeting with current team members, Strength and Conditioning Coaches, Athletic Training staff, NCAA Compliance Directors, and Academic Advisers.

The NCAA also mandates, *"An institution may not arrange miscellaneous, personalized recruiting aids (e.g., personalized jerseys) and may not permit a prospective student-athlete to engage in any game-day simulations (e.g., running onto the field with the team during pregame introductions) during an official visit. Personalized recruiting aids include any special additions to any location the prospective student-athlete will visit (e.g., locker room, coach's office, or arena) regardless of whether the items include the prospective student-athlete's name or picture."*

There are more than 300 pages of rules and restrictions in the NCAA compliance handbooks regarding recruiting procedures and campus visits, and there are many differences between sports and various levels. The information in this handbook is meant to be a resource and is not inclusive. If you are invited for an official campus visit, follow the direction of the athletic staff as to what is permissible during your visit.

Chris King, Director of Athletics at the University of Texas Rio Grande Valley, has spent 21 years in the sports industry. "My biggest pet peeve is when prospective student-athletes and/or parents who are on a campus recruiting visit meet with me and are unprepared. It is amazing to me the number of times recruits meet with me and seem disinterested, do not have questions to ask, or the worst, check their cell phones while I am providing them information about our department, sport program, and/or institution."

He adds, "As the Director of Athletics, I personally indicate to our head coach this is not a young man or woman that is a fit for our program or our culture. The disrespect for my time is not in the best interest for a prospective student-athlete who wants to enroll at our institution or receive an athletics scholarship. Prospective student-athletes and their families should treat the recruiting process and a campus visit like a job interview."

Judith M. Sweet has been an athletics administrator for more than 40 years. She is the former NCAA Senior VP and University of California San Diego Director of Athletics Emerita and serves as a gender equity consultant as well as the co-founder of the Alliance of Women Coaches (now called WeCOACH). She agrees that families should "do your homework in respect to what the college will mean to you for academics as well as athletics and social opportunities. Make sure that it's a good fit for your education in all ways."

13 QUESTIONS TO ASK

To stand out from the crowd, be prepared to ask the college coach questions. Coaches speak with literally hundreds of prospective students every year who all want athletic scholarships. Recruiting Coordinator and Rowing Coach Conny Kirsch, at the University of Central Florida, reinforces the idea that you need to do your research prior to a campus visit, "It's amazing to me that some recruits show up on a visit not knowing the names of the coaches on staff or their backgrounds and not having looked at the roster. Those are just things that baffle me."

Coaches use those conversations to evaluate maturity, commitment in the classroom, and leadership skills. Division III Head Cross Country Coach at Meredith College Leslie Payne describes a major pet peeve: "Recruits who talk about themselves the whole time and do not ask any questions about our program." It is essential to ask the coach questions to demonstrate your interest in the academic and athletic programs.

Here are some questions a student-athlete should ask a coach on the phone or in person:

1. What are the core values of your program?

Every coach should be able to rattle this off as quickly as their ABCs. If they can't, it may show a lack of vision for the program.

As a college coach, the acronym I used to describe our priorities was CIA: Character, Integrity, and Accountability. Character describes becoming who you are called to be; Integrity focuses on doing the right thing, especially when no one is watching, and Accountability emphasizes teammates and coaches holding everyone responsible for their actions.

Each coach will have their own values for their programs, but it is important to understand what their priorities are and if they are a good *fit*.

2. Why do you coach? What is your overall coaching philosophy?

This answer may seem rehearsed as coaches get asked this all the time. Hopefully, their passion for impacting lives will be evident. These questions can reveal a lot about their commitment to serve their student-athletes versus seeing them as chess pieces to win games.

3. What is a typical week like for an athlete in season? Out of season?

Most coaches will tell you about a typical practice schedule, but it's important to ask about things beyond actual practice time. What study hall hours are required for student-athletes as freshmen? What about weight training times? What are the expectations before and after practice in the training room, such as ice bath treatments? How often do you watch film? What about leadership development or mental skills training programs?

4. How do your student-athletes work through missed class time?

Most athletic departments will have a strict procedure of emails going to professors at the beginning of a semester regarding missed class time. However, it is typically the student's responsibility to make up work *prior* to traveling, unless a professor has agreed otherwise. Some professors may allow you to complete work online, and some rare instructors allow you to do it upon your return. You also should ask about academic resources available for student-athletes who might need a little extra help with their classes.

5. What challenges do you see as far as being a student-athlete with my major?

Depending on the university, some majors may not allow you to be an athlete for four years and complete your degree on time. Often, this happens with majors that are heavy in practicums/internships, especially in the junior and senior years. It may depend on the semester of your championship season (versus non-championship "training seasons") for your sport.

For example, are you a softball/baseball player who would be looking to student teach in the spring of your senior season? You need to research this, if you wish to major in nursing, education, athletic training, engineering, international business, or any program requiring an internship to graduate.

6. What are the needs for my recruiting class in terms of position and leadership?

This is a great question to see how interested a coach may be in you as an athlete and leader. It's important to understand the team dynamics for the year you join the team. For example, will they be graduating a lot of seniors the year before you would enter or after your freshman year? It could impact the success of the team and your potential playing time.

7. What role do you see me playing for the team as a freshman versus later in my career?

In theory, the last question would lead to the coach addressing your role. Do not ask, "Will I start?", as no coach can fully predict or want to promise that to you. (Be cautious if they do!) A variety of factors influence those decisions each season, including returning student-athletes, injuries, tactical decisions, and opponent match-ups. However, you should inquire about their overall plan from your freshman year until graduation.

8. Beyond high performance athletically and in the classroom, what intangibles are you looking for in a student-athlete?

By asking this question, you can demonstrate your maturity in understanding the bigger picture and what it means to be a good teammate beyond your athletic abilities. The response can give insight into what they value.

9. How should I handle the admissions process? Would I go directly through Admissions or through you? Which test do you prefer: ACT or SAT?

Most schools will want you to do the application process online through Admissions. During the summer and fall, that office often gets pummeled with applications, so many coaches keep a close eye on the processing of their recruits. It's best to let the coach know you have completed the application process, paperwork for financial aid, and submitted your test scores and transcripts. Do not depend on the coach to "get you accepted", as that is very rare and you still must meet the standards set by the Eligibility Centers for NAIA and NCAA DI and II.

10. What housing options do you recommend? Preferred locations? Living with other athletes?

There are typically specific housing placements for freshmen versus upperclassmen. Some coaches also look to house student-athletes together. On other campuses, student-athletes are encouraged to live with non-athletes to create some unique bonds outside of athletics.

11. What typical team-building activities does the team do each year?

The response to this will likely provide an understanding of the operating budgets of the program and how much they value team building. Some well-funded programs travel out of state for a few days of training during preseason. Most do one to two days of a retreat, a ropes course, and/or mental skills training early in their season.

12. What does the team do for fun on their days off?

While it is important for you to know the coach's answer to this question, it is also valuable for you to ask this of team members. How much does the team hang out together when it's not mandatory? What do they like to do? Try to get an understanding of how much of a priority "partying" is to the team when you interact with them, but be careful about asking a direct question. It could be misinterpreted as a priority to you.

13. What is the next step for me in the recruiting process?

This question sets up a proper way to let the coach be honest with you. If they have not seen your athletic abilities yet, they may ask you to attend an upcoming camp, or send your schedule or a video link. If they have seen you perform, and depending on your current year in school, they may want to get you through the application process or evaluate your eligibility.

If this is your first conversation with the college coach, *do not* ask about an athletic scholarship. You want the coach to walk away from your time together thinking you are a mature individual who

IF THIS IS YOUR FIRST CONVERSATION WITH THE COLLEGE COACH, DO NOT ASK ABOUT AN ATHLETIC SCHOLARSHIP.

is really investigating your options. Asking that one question about scholarships in an initial conversation makes a coach think that is your priority for choosing a school. While it may be a crucial factor for your decision, save it for later (unless the coach brings it up).

Other Important Aspects to Investigate...

1. Protocols for late-night arrivals back to campus.

How does the coaching staff handle returning from an away trip at night to ensure everyone's safety?

2. Campus crime statistics.

In the United States, these statistics must be published by law enforcement. The school typically can provide the information and address any concerns.

3. Designated parking.

If freshmen may have cars on campus, they are often assigned remote parking lots. On some larger campuses, they may need to take a bus to get from their designated parking to their residence halls.

4. The surrounding neighborhood and local attractions.

Drive around off campus at various times of the day. Does it feel comfortable and safe in this area? Visit local restaurants, movie theaters, malls, sporting venues, and other locations a student would likely go to on an evening or weekend.

5. Important health and safety considerations.

There is a wide spectrum of available medical attention, facilities, and resources on different campuses. While the athletic training room might not be your top spot to visit on campus, this could be a place where a student-athlete spends a lot of time if injured.

ATHLETIC TRAINING PERSONNEL AND FACILITIES

Quality certified athletic trainers (ATCs) are essential to helping student-athletes perform at their best. Deanna Rosato-Lewis is the Marketing Director of Sports Medicine for the Children's Hospital of New Orleans and been a Certified Athletic Trainer for ten years, working in both the NCAA Division I and at two Louisiana high schools. She recommends, "Get to know the ATCs working with your team. Ask questions related to vaccinations, physicals, medical releases, insurance coverage, billing, and physician care. The parents should know what doctors and hospitals the school works with, and what would happen if an injury happens on the road. These conversations can give a lot of peace of mind to parents."

Rosato-Lewis continues, "Some schools utilize graduate assistants; others have enough full-time staff. The key is to find out if the staff covering are in fact, certified athletic trainers or student trainers. A good relationship between the student-athlete and ATC is critical to success in athletics."

Arianne Davis is the former Head Athletic Trainer for Muskingum University and has over 15 years of experience, including in secondary schools, hospital orthopedics, and in bracing and casting, as well as coverage of NCAA Division I, II, and III programs. She suggests, "Tour the facilities! Count the things you see: Electrical modalities (ultrasound and electronic stim machines), treatment tables or taping tables, and whirlpool tanks. Fewer pieces of equipment mean there will be waiting times for treatment, especially when practice times overlap with other sports!"

While seeing the training room might not be a huge priority on a campus visit, ask any current student-athlete how much time they spend in these facilities daily doing treatments, cold tank recovery, and stretching! Their answers may surprise you!

CHAPTER 8

SPORTS CAMPS AND CLINICS

CONSIDERATIONS BEFORE PAYING CAMP TUITION

Many high school student-athletes receive invitations to college sports camps. These camps are often marketed as a way for prospects to "be seen" and be offered athletic scholarships. Other camps focus on instruction in skill development and on team tactics from high-level coaches. It's unlikely a student-athlete can attend all of them, so what is the best use of a limited budget?

I have mailed out thousands of camp invites over the years. Thanks to the marketing efforts of my hard-working assistants, most of my Identification (ID) Camps sold out within a few weeks of opening registration. In addition to running my own camps, I gained the perspective of many others as I worked on camp staffs for NCAA Division I schools in the ACC, SEC, Atlantic 10, and Colonial Athletic Association; NCAA Division II in the Rocky Mountain Athletic Conference; and NCAA Division III in the St. Louis Intercollegiate Athletic Conference.

Based on my extensive experience, the following are some areas to consider before swiping a credit card for camp tuition:

1. What Is Your Primary Objective in Attending a Sports Camp?

First, the student-athlete needs to decide what type of camp experience to have now versus later in high school. For those still in middle school or entering freshman year, a multiday summer camp experience is likely more focused on fun through skill development and tactics. However, if the primary objective is to bond with a team, the family should research a team camp setting.

For a camp that is truly geared toward helping a student-athlete earn a roster spot for a college team, investigate which ones are designed for coaches to see a student-athlete in various playing situations. Depending on the sport, some ID camps are geared toward that in a one- to two-day experience. It's important to note that not all college camps are geared toward this. Many larger camps simply shuttle hundreds of kids to various locations to get in their matches and are not focused on the college recruiting process.

For a camp where student-athletes are truly being evaluated by the coaching staff, research to see what the maximum number of participants is for the camp. Steve Swanson, the Head Women's Soccer Coach at the University of Virginia and United States Women's National Team Assistant, states, "A camp can be a great way to learn about the coaching staff, the program, and learn about the school. It's not just about being on the field. At a camp, you can glean a lot about the program and overall atmosphere. And from a coach's perspective, I can evaluate you athletically but more importantly, what kind of person you are."

2. Does the Camp Match My College Priorities?

Would this college still be right academically and socially? Research each college camp invitation to see if it meets your criteria. Just because a college coach sends a camp invite does not mean the college or even their program is the right fit. Remember also that a camp invite does not necessarily mean that college is recruiting you.

3. Interest Level of the College Coaching Staff

While the NCAA, NAIA, and other governing bodies do limit some levels of communication by college coaches to prospective student-athletes, there are ways to identify their interest level and whether attending a camp might be beneficial.

- Have their coaching staff members seen you compete live?

- If they couldn't communicate with you directly, did they discuss anything with your coaches or team managers? (Again, some sports and governing bodies allow this, while others do not so make sure you know the rules for your graduation year, sport, and college level.)

- Did you get an email in the first week after a recruiting showcase or did it take weeks before you heard from them?

- Finally, it is imperative you also investigate where the coaching staff is in their process for your recruiting class. Do they have you on their short list?

The coaches may be using camps to really take a good look at student-athletes. However, if you are early in your high school career, they simply may not be focused on evaluating that class quite yet. It often depends on simple manpower (the number of staff members), but every coaching staff has its own ways of recruiting.

For example, one NCAA DI head coach might focus on a short list of juniors and seniors, while assistants evaluate younger athletes. Yet, some head coaches do the exact opposite, especially if they have part-time assistants.

Every situation is unique, so it essential to note how much emphasis is placed on camps for a specific sport. For some college coaches, camps are their best recruiting tool, while other coaches do not even run camps. Emily Holsopple, North Carolina State University Rifle Head Coach, who previously spent four years at the US Olympic Training Center, offers some perspective on smaller roster teams, "Rifle is a bit more difficult to evaluate athletes. The sport has variations in the types of event (standing versus kneeling and prone), so we really evaluate what we currently see in the shooters and see what will transfer. We do not run camps per se, but many college campuses offer invitational 'open' matches which would allow a student-athlete to see the range on campus and they could set up a campus tour with the Admissions department."

Shortly after her lacrosse team won the NCAA Division II National Championship at Florida Southern College, Head Coach Kara Reber explained, "A camp provides an opportunity for me to not only focus on instruction and developing you as a player, but also a way for me to see if you are a good fit for our program overall. At a camp, I can see a lot more touches on the ball, as well as see the interactions you have with our coaching staff versus a limited amount of interaction and exposure at a recruiting event."

CHAPTER 9

APPLICATION PROCEDURES, FINANCIAL AID PROCESS, AND ATHLETIC SCHOLARSHIPS

APPLICATION PROCEDURES

It is imperative that student-athletes send in their applications as soon as the school opens enrollment. While schools can vary as to when they start accepting applications, the majority will open freshmen enrollment the summer prior to a student-athlete's senior year of high school. If a school has an early decision (ED) procedure, ask the coaching staff how this works with athletic offers. It is essential for student-athletes to check with the coaches recruiting them as to the best timeline and procedures to follow. Some helpful tips to make the application process go smoothly are the following:

1. **Inquire about the number and type of recommendation letters needed.**

Some schools require a reference from specific subject matter teachers or character references outside of the school. Ask if there is a specific form, or if it can be a general letter about the student-athlete. Request recommendation letters from high school counselors, teachers, coaches, bosses, and ministers very early as the most popular of these individuals get numerous requests and may take some time to get a letter back to you.

2. **Research the type of application and essay the school requires and the deadlines.**

Some schools will accept the Common Application and others will not. Some will require additional essays. Write on topics you are passionate about, and always have an English teacher look over it prior to sending!

3. **Inquire if the school requires an in-person or online interview.**

Many schools use interviews with enrollment staff and/or alumni to make admissions decisions.

4. **Research the test scores and GPA requirements.**

Student-athletes should take their initial ACT/SAT tests by the fall of their junior year, if not earlier. While the general student population often takes these tests during the spring of their junior year or even senior year, there are many benefits for student-athletes in taking them earlier. For example, if a student-athlete's ACT/SAT test scores do not meet the standard requirements, they should retake the tests, as many schools *super score* (use the highest score for a specific subject area from

DO NOT EXPECT THE COACH WILL JUST "GET ME IN".

various testing dates). Also, taking these tests earlier will allow coaches to decide about a student-athlete earlier, knowing their scores will likely increase.

Do not expect the coach will just "get me in". Many years ago, this practice was commonplace in athletics, but it is very rare now. Therefore, student-athletes should not have this expectation and should plan for meeting the minimum requirements published by the college.

5. Request official transcripts and test scores be sent directly to each college as soon as junior year grades are posted.

Many high schools have limited summer hours. Request transcripts be sent as soon as junior year grades are posted so there is not a delay in processing. Student-athletes should be proactive in the process and keep in constant contact with the coach. Some colleges will want application materials to be sent to the admissions office, while others will want the documents sent to the coaches directly, so it is best to ask about the institution's procedures.

FINANCIAL AID PROCESS

Derry Ebert, Vice President for Enrollment Management at Warner University, has spent 20 years working in admissions in Colorado, Kansas, and Florida, and offers this advice, "My words of wisdom when it comes to families seeing the cost of tuition is not to be scared by 'sticker shock'. It is like buying a car—no one really pays the sticker price."

1. Investigate the process of applying for scholarships beyond athletics, especially for NCAA Division III.

Jason Davis, Cross Country and Track and Field Coach at Marietta College in Ohio, states, "Everyone always wants to know how much athletic scholarship money the school can offer. While this doesn't apply to all sports or programs, with Division III, we can't offer athletic scholarships, so families should look into all types of scholarships. However, for us to offer a roster spot, they must have applied and been accepted. They need to visit and show strong interest. I might make an offer a bit earlier if in competition with a conference team, but we like to really know the recruit before we make an offer of a roster spot."

2. Submit the Free Application for Federal Student Aid (FAFSA).

It is an essential part of the process to see what need-based loans, grants, and scholarships are available from the federal government and, for some colleges, also from the state. The FAFSA can be filed during the fall of senior year of high school and is based on the parents' prior year's taxes.

3. Understand how financial aid and tuition discounts work for the college.

Depending on the sport and division of the college, they may or may not be able to stack athletic, academic, and independent/ community scholarships. Ask how this works at each college the student-athlete is applying to, since it varies across schools.

Carrie Doyle, Senior Associate Athletics Director for Compliance at North Carolina State University, states, "Parents need to understand upfront that NCAA rules may mean they need to choose either the athletics scholarship or institutional aid (depending on the sport and division, they may or may not be allowed to keep both). Most institutional financial aid 'counts' as athletics aid, which cuts into the athletics aid a coach may want to give to other recruits. A coach is trying to help develop the best package of financial aid for the recruit, while maximizing the amount of athletics aid to also be used to recruit other talented players."

4. Apply for independent scholarships.

Make sure you are investigating all types of scholarships available. Check out www.fastweb.com, www.scholarships.com, and www. studentscholarshipssearch.com. Also, check with local community groups such as Kiwanis, the Boy and Girl Scouts, credit unions, banks, churches, and local businesses.

ATHLETIC SCHOLARSHIPS

I love the movie The Blindside, *but it gives an impression that college coaches are going to be pounding down your door offering full athletic scholarships just because you are talented. I think that's a false representation of what the college recruiting process looks like for about 95 percent of student-athletes.*

Barry King, the Head Coach of Men's and Women's Water Polo at George Washington University, warns families about placing too much emphasis on athletic scholarships. "First and foremost, the system is rigged for disappointment. A lot of time is put into building the relationship with the prospect and then at the end, a value must be put on that relationship. Agreement on that value is rare. Every scholarship offer has its own nuance and set of parameters."

Carrie Doyle, Senior Associate Athletics Director for Compliance at North Carolina State University, further explains the various dimensions of an athletic offer, "A financial aid agreement is the kind of document you absolutely *have to* read and understand. Coaches may offer a percentage of a scholarship, but what is it the percentage of? Total cost of attendance or what a full scholarship used to be (tuition, fees, room, board, and books)? Is the agreement a multiyear agreement with zero scholarship dollars in one or more years, or is it a one-year agreement? Sometimes coaches will say, 'I'll cover your costs,' which generally means something less than a scholarship covering the total cost of attendance."

Some smaller colleges are more likely to offer a partial athletic scholarship or a walk-on position. *So, falling in love with lower student-professor ratios in an academic major, a smaller friendlier campus, and an awesome athletic opportunity may mean finding a way to pay for this great opportunity.*

Some families think they can just ask the coach or financial aid office for a better offer. But it's complicated. It depends on the circumstances. Typically, unless the Estimated Family Contribution (EFC) changes for some special circumstances (as evaluated through the FAFSA), it is highly unlikely to change an offer much beyond $500–$2000. It is a delicate conversation to have with a coach, so be cautious to not seem ungrateful for a current offer.

Kathy DeBoer, the Executive Director of the American Volleyball Coaches Association (AVCA), states, "It always amazes me when a parent says, 'She has to get an athletic scholarship because we can't pay for her to go to college.' It's not financial aid, that's a different program—you don't apply for these scholarships—whether music or athletic—you earn it. There is a huge difference. Most kids don't have the skills, training, mental toughness, or physical attributes to earn these."

Almost every coach *wants* to give out a full scholarship to recruits, *but...* they only have a certain "pot" of money to use across the whole team, which is based on regulations issued by the governing body, their conference, and the school. Many athletic programs are not even fully funded to the conference maximums or what the governing body allows. This is simply because the institution decides how much aid will be used for athletics. If not fully funded, that coach may not be happy about it, but can do little to change it. Coaches must find ways to make their allotment work across their whole team. For sports with equivalency requirements, this can be even more challenging. It's not that they don't think a student-athlete deserves more athletic scholarship money, it's that they simply don't have it available.

CHAPTER 10

DECISIONS, DECISIONS, DECISIONS

"Coach, I just want an opportunity to continue playing in college."

It was April of her high school senior year when I received an email describing a young lady's desire to play college athletics. She was not looking for an athletic scholarship. She made it clear she knew she probably was not at the same talent level as our current student-athletes. Her email noted she already had been accepted into the college and inquired if there were any walk-on positions for the upcoming fall season.

I checked with Admissions and saw her outstanding academic record. The difficulty was that we typically had our recruits verbally committed to us late in their junior year of high school (or right after our summer camps prior to senior year). I really did not need another player for her position, but I asked for some game film. After watching some video, I invited her to come for a tryout where she did well.

*I made it clear that we did not have any athletic scholarship money for her. She said she wanted to work hard to make herself better and encourage her teammates while getting a quality education. Playing time was not expected by her or her parents. **I could tell her desire and positive attitude were contagious; she was an innate leader and was disciplined in her academics.** Her high school coaches echoed the same things and spoke highly of her work ethic and character. I decided to take a chance. Years later, she had her "Rudy" moment when she made an amazing game-altering play for her team in a challenging situation!*

Athletes considering walking-on to a program need to make sure the college is great fit *in all* aspects besides athletics: Academic, social, location, and financial. If all those areas line up, there are a few other aspects of being a non-scholarship athlete to consider.

WHAT DOES IT TAKE TO BE A WALK-ON?

Time Commitment

Understand the time commitment required. Find out what the practice, game, film, weights, study hall, and travel schedules look like in a typical week. Are the sacrifices worth it?

ARE THE SACRIFICES WORTH IT?

"We" Versus "Me" Mentality

Being a walk-on typically means not seeing the field, court, track, or competition mat beyond practice. That means helping support teammates even when not playing. It is important for a walk-on to maintain a positive attitude and be hardworking every day. This includes accepting the coaching staff's decisions without complaining.

Some schools don't always travel their whole team, especially when class time would be missed, and someone isn't expected to play. Other programs may not even give a walk-on a uniform on game day. This is not always the case, but can be a challenging situation if a walk-on is not mentally prepared for it.

Other Considerations:

- Does the coach know anything about the student-athlete? Has the coach seen the student-athlete compete prior to enrolling in the school?

- Will the coach still consider cutting the student-athlete during preseason? Do they ever "redshirt" (meaning purposely not pulling a player in a game freshman year)?

- What has the coaching staff done in the past with walk-ons? Are they treated the same as the rest of the team?

- Research the Intramural and/or club opportunities at the school versus playing at the college varsity level.

VERBAL COMMITMENTS AND OFFICIAL SIGNING

It is imperative for families to understand the difference between a verbal commitment and officially signing for a roster position. Verbal commitments are not binding, but it is essential to take them seriously as coaches' jobs literally depend on their recruiting classes getting committed. Student-athletes **should not** take verbal commitments lightly and think they can still be searching for a better offer while verbally committed to a college. This is a bad practice and demonstrates a lack of integrity. The college coaching circles are very small and well connected. It is highly likely this practice of still "shopping around" will get back to college coaches and a student-athlete will potentially lose all opportunities.

Marty English, Defensive Coordinator and Linebacker Coach at the University of Northern Colorado, says he "does not like student-athletes who verbally commit and then back out. I do not like when they are playing games with multiple coaches on signing dates. They need to take a commitment seriously."

The purpose of the National Letter of Intent (NLI) program for NCAA DI and DII is to provide a written binding commitment between both the institution and the prospective student-athlete, to provide the prospective student-athlete with athletic financial aid, and to end the recruiting process. The NAIA signs a Letter of Intent (LOI).

The NLI is intended for prospective student-athletes who are in position to enroll at a four-year institution for the upcoming fall term. The NLI is signed by a high school senior and is ONLY for those who are receiving an offer of athletic aid for NCAA. While those walking-on to an athletic program (no athletic aid) may sign a commitment letter, the NLI is specifically for those receiving athletic aid.

Prospective student-athletes attending two-year colleges or prep schools can also sign an NLI prior to their four-year college enrollment. This does not apply to four-year college transfers. The NLI policies are the same for all sports, but the signing dates are different.

According to Susan Peal, NCAA Director of Governance of the National Letter of Intent Program, common NLI policies to be aware of are the following:

1. Once an NLI is signed, coaches from other institutions must cease communication with the prospective student-athlete and family.

2. Once an NLI is signed with one division (e.g., Division II), the prospective student-athlete cannot sign another NLI or be recruited by another division (e.g., Division I).

3. A prospective student-athlete *can* sign an NLI before they are admitted to the signing institution and before having an initial eligibility decision.

4. The NLI is a written binding commitment. A verbal commitment is not binding. This means the prospective student-athlete or institution does not have to honor a verbal commitment.

"What Does Committing to an Athletic Program Really Mean?"

We've all heard about a student-athlete committing to a college and getting a "full ride" athletic scholarship. But what does that term "committing" really mean? Does it come on signing day at the high school? When accepting a financial aid package? Or on the phone with a college coach?

Verbal commitments can be made by both a coach and a student-athlete. Unfortunately, with the rise of early recruiting, more families are feeling pressure to commit early. Then, once a high school or club team member commits early, it becomes a domino effect (panic spreads across the rest of the team). Do not verbally commit to a school unless it is 100 percent the right *fit* for you. Decommitting to a school, or verbally committing while still "shopping around", tends not to turn out well.

DO NOT VERBALLY COMMIT TO A SCHOOL UNLESS IT IS 100 PERCENT THE RIGHT FIT FOR YOU. DECOMMITTING TO A SCHOOL, OR VERBALLY COMMITTING WHILE STILL "SHOPPING AROUND", TENDS NOT TO TURN OUT WELL.

For NCAA colleges, student-athletes cannot currently officially sign until their senior year. There are a lot of proposals being debated, so this timetable may change. Before agreeing to a written commitment, follow these specific steps:

1. **Register with the Eligibility Center.**

As previously discussed, register on the website and have official test scores and transcripts sent as well.

2. **Know about the athletic, academic, location, and social environment.**

Have all the questions mentioned earlier been answered?

3. **Visit the college while students are on campus.**

Remember all those fancy college brochures piled up on the kitchen counter? They are designed by marketing specialists to show all the positives about the colleges and minimize the negatives. Make sure to look for the good and the not-so-great parts of the school. If a coach never takes a recruit into the locker room, it's probably awful inside!

4. Apply and be accepted to the college.

Before signing, the student-athlete should complete the application process. Most colleges will expect this process to be completed senior year. Athletic scholarship offers can be withdrawn if the admissions process isn't completed by a certain date.

5. Know EXACTLY how much the academic scholarships, athletic scholarships, and financial aid cover.

In conjunction with a completed FAFSA, make sure everything is in writing. Do not rely on verbal commitments. Most athletic scholarships are typically one-year renewable scholarships, NOT automatic four-year scholarships. Be sure to get answers to all these important questions:

- Which meal plan is specifically included?

- What about books, computer, and science lab fees?

- Who is responsible for any sports fees?

- How much do tuition and fees typically increase each year?

- What GPA must be maintained to keep an academic scholarship?

- How do injuries impact an athletic scholarship long term?

- Could increases or decreases of athletic scholarships be dependent upon athletic performance?

College personnel interact with literally hundreds of recruits a year so it is imperative that families initiate these steps and not just assume the coach or admissions staff will address them.

SIGNING DAY

As high school students and their families anticipate the exciting day of signing, it's critical to be aware of the actual procedures.

First, understand that anything verbally agreed upon prior to a signing date is just that, a verbal commitment. Still, student-athletes should take the process of verbal commitments extremely serious. Despite the dramatic situations often play out on television, last-minute decisions are few and far between. Typically, most student-athletes have verbally committed to a university a few months or even years ahead and are just waiting for the official signing date.

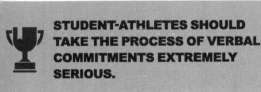

STUDENT-ATHLETES SHOULD TAKE THE PROCESS OF VERBAL COMMITMENTS EXTREMELY SERIOUS.

1. **Various signing periods depend on the sport and competition level.**

Families often become anxious when they see another student-athlete sign and they do not have their own paperwork yet. Just because a friend in a different sport and competition level is signing at a certain time, does not mean these are the dates everyone will sign. Specific dates change every year, so student-athletes should consult the website of the governing body for the specific sport and institution.

2. **Governing bodies differ in terms of signing dates and policies.**

NCAA Division I and II scholarship student-athletes can sign an NLI with a financial aid agreement. NCAA Division III student-athletes can sign commitment letters and financial aid agreements. Ivy Leagues, which can't offer athletic aid, have a separate procedure. NAIA prospects can sign Letters of Intent (LOI), and the NJCAA,

NCCAA, and USCAA all have their own steps for signings. Detailing the signing dates and policies of every governing body and sport would triple the length of this book, so consult their websites!

3. **A National Letter of Intent (NCAA DI & II) must be accompanied by a written financial aid agreement.**

To be valid, the NLI must spell out the specific terms of athletic scholarships being awarded. Often, people refer to the offer of a "full ride." Some of that may be academic scholarships, grants, and other financial aid combined with athletic scholarships. Also, it may only be for tuition and *not* room and board or other costs of attendance (books, student fees, activity fees, travel, etc.). Sometimes, this financial aid will only list a percentage of tuition, housing, and student fees, as final tuition numbers haven't been determined by the college. Know *exactly* how much will be owed after the athletic scholarship is applied. Do not assume that 100 percent of tuition includes books, housing, meals, and student fees. In reality, a tiny percentage of student-athletes receive a full ride.

4. **A NLI is an agreement with the university and NOT with a specific coach.**

Current legislation states that even though an NLI is signed by the Athletic Director and/or Compliance Director, the commitment is to that institution even if a coach leaves a school. (There are some proposals to change this legislation.)

5. **A NLI is LEGALLY BINDING.**

It is challenging to get out of an NLI. In one extreme situation, a student-athlete was able to get out of her commitment letter to a school across the country. She had multiple deaths in the family within two months of her signing date and wanted to stay closer to home. She had to go through a lengthy and difficult appeals process to get released. A student-athlete changing their mind is not a reason for a release.

6. Failure to complete one full academic year will have penalties.

The NLI terms include, "*I understand that if I do not attend the institution named in this document for one full academic year and I enroll in another institution participating in the NLI program, I may not compete in intercollegiate athletics until I have completed one full academic year in residence at the latter institution. Further, I understand I shall be charged with the loss of one season of intercollegiate athletics competition in all sports. This is in addition to any seasons of competition used at any institutions.*" It is imperative student-athletes do not take this commitment lightly as there are many short- and long-term implications for their athletic careers.

7. Signing parties vary across schools and sports organizations.

High schools (and sometimes travel clubs) vary in terms of how much they recognize student-athlete commitments. Contact the athletic director, coaches, principals, or club directors regarding any public celebration of accomplishments. Some student-athletes have chosen to celebrate with just their family at home, while other schools or clubs may include local media. Depending on when a ceremony is scheduled, the student-athlete may have to "pretend" to sign documents for the media because they were already completed *prior to the ceremony*.

8. NCAA coaches cannot hand-deliver signing papers or be present for a signing day ceremony.

NCAA legislation prevents coaches from physically delivering the signing documents. Instead, the paperwork is typically mailed or emailed a few days prior to a signing period. These NCAA college coaches cannot be present during a signing, even for highly recruited athletes. However, coaches from other governing bodies may attend signing parties.

9. **NCAA coaches cannot publicly comment about recruits to the media until *after* the NLI documents have been submitted.**

Local media outlets will often request comments from a college coach regarding a recruit's future contributions to a program. The information may only be released to the press once all documentation has been completed with the NCAA and the university. This includes all school and coach social media platforms as well.

IMPORTANT STEPS AFTER SIGNING

The congratulatory high fives, pats on the back, and photo ops have tapered off, and the focus is on high school graduation! With the signing of a National Letter of Intent (NCAA DI or DII), Letter of Intent (NAIA), or other financial package to join a college program and receive an athletic scholarship, the commitment is official. So now, besides some more press interviews, it's all smooth sailing until August, right? Wrong!

I Signed . . . Now What?

1. **All other recruiters need to be notified.**

This should be completed after a verbal commitment, but if it wasn't, the student-athlete needs to contact each coach to let them know of their decision. To avoid violating any recruiting ethics, the student-athlete needs to make it explicitly clear in writing to both admissions and the coaching staff of every college they have interacted with during the recruiting process. Because of relationships formed during the process, it's better to call some coaches directly.

National Championship Head Lacrosse Coach at Florida Southern College Kara Reber advised, "If you have committed somewhere else just tell me. Just respond to an email saying you are not interested in my school. Don't just avoid me. I get 'broken' up with all the time."

It is important to not burn any bridges during these conversations. First, you want to leave a good impression of a club or high school program for those younger players who may wish to pursue the same college. Second, circumstances can change down the road, which could mean transferring to a different college.

2. Do not let "senioritis" take over.

It's common for a student-athlete to just want the whole high school thing to be over and head off to college. However, graduation from high school is essential, and many academic scholarships and admissions standards *consider all academic semesters*. Also, coaches really do care about this as it demonstrates your work ethic and commitment.

3. Make sure there's full acceptance into the university.

Many student-athletes have the impression that since they have signed with the college, they do not have to complete any other part of the application process. However, that is not the case. If there's no acceptance letter in hand from the admissions department, contact them immediately to find out what steps are needed to complete the process.

4. Plan another visit to the college prior to attending.

After signing, ask the coaching staff and admissions personnel about orientation. Some schools host an official visit after signing, while others will do it prior to signing. Many schools only offer unofficial visits, which means families cover the cost of the trip. Remember, coaches are juggling a lot of recruits, so it's up to each student-athlete to take the initiative to investigate what the school requires. Every college handles this process in its own way, so ask the coach directly.

5. Complete all other necessary paperwork for the college.

Some colleges require the student-athlete to apply for housing and meet with an academic adviser to plan out classes. Most institutions will expect that the FAFSA is completed to see if there's qualification for any other aid, like scholarships, grants, or loans. Some schools mandate a deposit for housing or for registering for classes.

There will also be medical paperwork to complete for the school and for the athletic department. Many schools require a physical and a test for sickle cell anemia prior to competing. Check with the college about their specific procedures; some bring in doctors during preseason and others expect the completion of paperwork with a family doctor prior to the student's attendance.

6. Research if retaking the ACT/SAT tests might result in more academic or community scholarships.

Just a few points can often help a student-athlete reach a different tier of academic scholarship allotment. Ask the Admissions or Financial Aid office if an increase of a few points could make a difference.

7. Make sure final transcripts and any updated test scores are sent to both the university and the Eligibility Center (NCAA or NAIA).

If playing NCAA DI, DII, or NAIA, student-athletes will need to make sure all documents are completed and submitted for final certification from the governing body during the summer.

8. NCAA student-athletes need to make sure they request final amateurism certification.

Initial registration with the NCAA Eligibility Center includes some basic questions about amateurism status. This often happens early in the high school career, so it *must* be revisited after April 1 of the student-athlete's senior year.

9. Make good choices on social media and in the community.

The college *does not* have to honor the commitment letter if the student-athlete gets into trouble with the law or makes poor choices on social media platforms that disrespect individuals, the athletic department, or the university.

10. Prepare both mentally and physically for the next level.

Ask about getting a summer workout plan from the coaching staff. To help student-athletes get acclimated, some NCAA DI programs enroll them during the summer and sometimes even spring if they have graduated early. Finally, ask about any other requirements (reading books or watching specific movies on topics of leadership and teamwork) prior to entering their program.

BEING A COLLEGE STUDENT-ATHLETE CAN BE AN AMAZING EXPERIENCE. IF YOU THINK YOU HAVE THE TALENT TO PLAY AT THE NEXT LEVEL, DO YOUR RESEARCH USING THE "BROKEN LEG TEST".

Being a college student-athlete can be an amazing experience. If you think you have the talent to play at the next level, do your research using the "Broken Leg Test", initiate emails with video links to coaches, and go find the right fit for you to live your dream! Make sure you take the right steps now to create the best scenarios for the student-athlete!

Don't ever let someone tell you, you can't do something.
Not even me. You got a dream, you got to protect it.
When people can't do something themselves, they want
to tell you, that you can't do it.
You want something, go get it. Period.

—Will Smith (as Chris Gardner) The Pursuit of Happyness

Still have questions regarding the college recruiting process? Email us at info@lookingforafullride.com or visit our free recruiting blogs at www.rlopezcoaching.com

GLOSSARY

AAU—Amateur Athletic Union aausports.org

ACT/SAT—college entrance exams www.collegeboard.org

AVCA—American Volleyball Coaches Association www.avca.org

DA—Development Academies (soccer) www.ussoccerda.com

ECNL—Elite Clubs National League (soccer)
    www.eliteclubsnationalleague.com

ED—Early Decision for college acceptance

EFC—Estimated Family Contribution for Financial Aid studentaid.
    ed.gov/sa/fafsa

FAFSA—Free Application for Federal Student Aid for US students
    studentaid.ed.gov/sa/fafsa

HUDL—tool to upload game film www.hudl.com

IRL—Institutional Request List (for NCAA coaches)
    www.ncaa.org/student-athletes

LOI—Letter of Intent, NAIA official signing documents naia.org

NAIA—National Association of Intercollegiate Athletics /naia.org

NAYS—National Alliance for Youth Sports www.nays.org

NCAA—National Collegiate Athletic Association
    www.ncaa.org/student-athletes

NCCAA—National Christian College Athletic Association
    thenccaa.org

NJCAA—National Junior College Athletic Association njcaa.org

NLI—National Letter of Intent, NCAA DI and II official signing
    documents www.nationalletter.org

PSA—Prospective Student-Athlete www.ncaa.org/student-athletes

QU—app to upload game film

TOEFL—Test of English as a Foreign Language www.ets.org/toefl

USCAA—US Collegiate Athletic Association www.theuscaa.com

USOTC—United States Olympic Training Center www.teamusa.org

USWNT—United States Women's National Team (soccer)
www.ussoccer.com

For more information, contact info@lookingforafullride.com

RESOURCES
AUTHOR
RECOMMENDS

C.A.R.E.™

College Athlete Recruiting Education

a new era for student-athletes & their families to

GET EDUCATED & BUILD A STRATEGY TO

GET RECRUITED

Learn more & book your spot on C.A.R.E.™ today at

CollegeAthleteRecruiting.US

broadcasting athletes

C.A.R.E.™
College Athlete Recruiting Education
powered by QU

GET IN THE
GAME

FCA IS ENGAGING, EQUIPPING, AND EMPOWERING COACHES AND ATHLETES TO KNOW JESUS CHRIST AND HELP OTHERS DO THE SAME

JOIN YOUR LOCAL FCA STAFF IN THIS WORK:
www.FCA.org/find-your-local-staff

FCA.org | FCAcamps.org | fca@fca.org
The heart and soul in sports®